MW01071480

Become tne Leader
You'd Love to Follow

PRACTICAL MEDITATIONS ON
CRAFTING VISION,
BUILDING ALIGNMENT,
& DRIVING EXECUTION

Dr. Stephen Julian
& Timothy Parsons

Copyright © 2018 by Dr. Stephen Julian and Timothy Parsons. All rights reserved.

No part of this book may be reproduced or utilized in any form or by any means, electric or mechanical, including photocopying, recording, or by information storage or retrieval system, without permission in writing from the authors.

Everything DiSC Work of Leaders® and Everything DiSC® Management are registered trademarks of John Wiley & Sons, Inc., or its affiliated companies.

Table of Contents

Dedication

Stephen: To Judy, you've inspired me to be a better leader.

Tim: To Missy, it is finally finished and has just begun…

Authors, Audience, and Purpose

This book has two authors, Stephen and Tim, but for the sake of our reader the chapters are written in the first person. Its principles and ideas reflect the training and experiences we each bring to this project. Stephen has a background in philosophy and communication, with experience as a college professor and administrator, consultant and coach, and, for a brief period, local church pastor. Tim's education is in psychology and theology with experience as a family counselor, pastor, and college student services expert.

You are our audience if you fall into one of three categories: 1) You are a leader as defined within the pages of this book, 2) You are seeking to determine whether you are a leader and are willing to discover that you may be an influencer, but not a leader, and 3) You are looking to identify an appropriate leader to follow.

We are looking for leaders who want to be challenged, cognitively and behaviorally, in each of the five areas around which this book is organized: The leader's character, The leader's role - crafting vision, The leader's role - building alignment, The leader's role - driving execution, and The leader's success. We are not selling a product (e.g., "The Leader's Guide to Making Millions") or a process (e.g., "Three Easy Steps to Becoming a Leader") but are asking you to consider how you fit within a framework of leadership that emphasizes the leader's character, role, and success. This book is meant to encourage your growth in both thought and practice.

Additionally, this book will help you to determine whether you are, in fact, a leader in the sense we describe. It may reveal that you are an influencer of others without having to be a leader who pursues the work of vision, alignment, and execution. I have someone I love dearly who has self-identified as a follower more than as a leader, while still being a significant influencer of others. It may be this conflation of influence with leadership that has encouraged the "everyone's a leader" perspective.

Finally, you may need to identify a leader worth following. This book will help you to recognize leaders you'd love to follow and should be following.

There are thousands of books on leadership. Some are theory-laden, while others are more practically oriented. This book falls into the latter camp. The chapters are intentionally brief - meditations more than fully-developed treatises on particular topics. In some instances, the tone is meant to be provocative, to take a stance that will engage the reader at the level of values and perspective. We are less concerned that you agree, than that you engage and that that engagement leads to growth, both professional and personal. To that end, each chapter concludes with a series of questions. If you'll take time to meditate on the principles and to consider the practical implications for your life and development, and then to identify specific behaviors to adopt, strengthen, or avoid as a result, we will have achieved our purpose.

Each chapter has a consistent format: Title, principle, content, and questions. The questions are intended to be open-ended, serving as prompts for further reflection or other questions that may come to mind.

You may choose to read this book with a partner, discussing the principles and questions, and then holding one another accountable to behavioral growth. My dad used to tell me: "If you read a book and get one thing out of it, it was worth reading." I've read some very long and complex books to find that one takeaway. Our hope is that you will find several insights of value in these pages, but that, at the very least, you will find your one thing.

More specifically, this is our hope for you: May you become the leader you'd love to follow as you interact with these growth-provoking meditations.

Introduction

What Is a Leader?

What is a leader? Who is a leader? Should you lead? Do you have a choice?

In the simplest sense, a leader is someone with followers. It is popular these days to embrace slogans such as "Everyone a leader." But just as saying that every home is dysfunctional empties the category of functional homes, so saying that everyone is a leader renders vacuous the distinction between those who lead and those who follow. When I was asked to address a group of nurses on the topic, "Everyone a leader," I was hesitant until I was told that these were nurses who had been selected as leaders from among their teams and organizations. Even so, looking back, I imagine that many audience members were actually managers more than leaders. What's the difference?

I will adopt a definition of "leader" that, while simple, retains significance worth exploring. Everything DiSC is a suite of personality assessments developed by John Wiley & Sons. This suite contains both Everything DiSC Work of Leaders® and Everything DiSC® Management. To distinguish these roles, Wiley defines leading as a one-to-many relationship, while managing is a one-to-one relationship. That is, leaders lead groups and managers manage individuals. Then Wiley identifies the work of leaders and distinguishes that from the role of managers. Leaders are responsible for three things: 1) Crafting vision, 2) Building alignment, and 3) Driving execution. Managers perform four functions: 1) Direct and delegate, 2) Motivate, 3) Develop, and 4) Manage up to their managers. Finally, Wiley identifies eight leadership styles associated with the DiSC model (where D stands for "dominance," i for "influence," S for "steadiness," and C for "conscientiousness"). Those eight styles are Pioneering, Energizing, Affirming, Inclusive, Humble, Deliberate, Resolute, and Commanding.

This distinction between leading and managing has a number of benefits. It provides a rationale for each role as essential to the success and well-being of any organization, addressing both the group and the individual. Therefore, both roles have value. Today's emphasis on leading often privileges the leader over the manager and makes leading the preferable pursuit. The challenge is that few individuals are equally gifted in the activities associated with leading and managing. Most people, if they can be developed as a leader or manager, are better at one.

Even within either role, people are not proficient at each of the required elements. Leaders and managers are never complete in themselves but rely on the strengths and gifting of others to enhance their shared success. This reminder of interdependence is necessary as a counterweight to our culture's subtle emphasis on omnicompetence (i.e., seeking to be skilled in everything so that one need not rely on others).

So, a leader is someone who guides the efforts of the many by crafting a vision, building alignment around that vision, and then driving execution of the behaviors needed to realize the vision. Is everyone a leader? No. Should you lead? Leadership is a high calling and should be pursued by those who have the desire, drive, and ability to develop the necessary character and behaviors. I would contend that some people are born leaders. Some people are developed as leaders. Most people should seek to follow commendable leaders.

This book has five sections, with the middle three corresponding to the "work of leaders" (Vision/Alignment/Execution). I begin with the leader's character and conclude with the leader's success.

This book is intended for you who are pursuing the calling of leadership and challenges you to become the leader you'd love to follow. Perhaps working through the topics and questions in each chapter will confirm that you are a leader and will help you to identify areas for growth. Perhaps you will realize that you are not a leader, but an influencer and reading these chapters will better enable you to identify those leaders you'd love to follow, someone you respect and whose vision you'd love to help make real. Find your calling, be it leader or follower, and pursue it. Become the leader you'd love to follow or learn to find the leader you need to follow. We believe that either outcome has value and will serve as a reward for the time you invest reading and reflecting on these pages.

Section 1

The Leader's Character

The relationship between leadership and character is complex. Some would argue that if a person fulfills his organizational functions effectively, personal morality is something altogether separate. But many types of organizations are built on the integrity of leadership (e.g., ministry, education, financial advisors - just to name a few) and the professional/personal distinction easily crumbles. These chapters look at the need for leaders to examine the perceptions of their character and to act in ways that increase effectiveness through the preservation of positive perceptions.

"A Blessing and a Curse" challenges the strong leader to exercise strength with maturity.

"Humility's Freedoms" discusses the ways in which acting with humility gains access to freedoms that might otherwise remain out of reach.

"An Antidote to Regret" examines strategies for regret minimization.

"An Estate of Pearls" looks at legacy and the principles a leader passes to the next generation as an inheritance of wisdom.

"Protecting the Value of Your Name" reminds the leader that a good name lost is nearly impossible to recover.

As you read these meditations, consider your character and its impact on your effectiveness as a leader.

Chapter 1

Self-neutering is painful and unproductive.

A Blessing and a Curse

My children love the television show Monk. Monk is an obsessive-compulsive detective who sees his unusual powers of observation as both a blessing and a curse. Many leaders with whom I work have strong personalities. Those personalities have enabled them to influence others and are one reason they naturally gravitate toward leadership roles. But many of them find this strength of personality to be both a blessing and a curse. This is not to say that those with less move-to-the-front personalities cannot be effective leaders. It is to say that they face different challenges.

Recently I met with two leaders who share responsibilities in guiding a team. Both women, one is more direct and forceful and the other is more indirect and reflective. The less direct leader pointed out that during recent team meetings she had taken a back seat and allowed her colleague to lead the discussions even when those discussions focused on her areas of leadership. As they discussed this situation, they concluded that both were to blame. The strong leader finds it easy to fill the void when the indirect leader hesitates and doesn't step forward. The indirect leader knows that the two of them have discussed the situation and agree about what should be done and that her more outspoken colleague is doing a fine job presenting their viewpoint to the team.

Two problems that emerge in this situation:

1. The strong leader is perceived by team members as running roughshod over the more introverted partner.

2. The more introverted leader is failing to be identified with her areas of responsibility, potentially begging the question: Why is she needed in this role?

Three realities strong leaders must face:

1. While both leaders share responsibility for how things played out in front of the team, it is the strong leader who typically is singled out for blame. People see her as bullying her fellow leader, when in reality, both have contributed to this situation. The best solution is for the quieter leader to tell the team what has happened, to assure team members that the leaders are on the same page and that they will continue working to share leadership appropriately and effectively.

2. People often feel the need to protect others from strong leaders, even when those leaders are mature, emotionally aware, and empathetic. They are simply more direct, and

that directness is often interpreted as inappropriate when it may be expressed in an entirely appropriate fashion. The world is not fair and so strong leaders must be prepared to be misinterpreted. This happens, in part, when they have worked with team members for many years and their immature behaviors from the past color the lens through which their current behaviors are interpreted.

3. Strong leaders, if honest, often **do** believe that they can say and do things better than others. If they are wise, they know that they cannot do the work of an entire team and that the people around them bring differing, genuine, valuable strengths. Others may not be as efficient or productive as they are, but may bring people skills, creative insights, willingness to persist in detailed work that requires attention to precision, and other strengths needed by the team; strengths these leaders cannot provide.

<u>**Four strategies**</u> **strong leaders should adopt to maximize their effectiveness:**

1. Remember, when tempted to think they can do it all better and faster, there are many times when this simply cannot be true.

2. Make sure they are selective in the expression of their strength of personality. Become better listeners and allow others to lead differently, but in ways that influence the team for good.

3. Don't learn the wrong lesson. Don't bury your strength to avoid being misinterpreted by others. You must risk others not understanding if you are to fully express your strengths.

4. Realize that how results are achieved does matter. Allow other leaders to direct their areas of responsibility, even when they are slower to speak, less forceful in expression, and bring about less dramatic results. Teamwork is about results achieved by a group that could not be achieved by an individual.

Like Monk, the strong leader's tendency to speak up and to direct can be both a blessing and a curse. The real work begins when the strong leader becomes self-aware and realizes that his strength can quickly turn into lost opportunities and stunted growth if he doesn't learn how to wield it effectively.

Questions to consider:

1. Are you a strong leader? Are you maturing in the expression of that strength?

2. Are you fully persuaded that you need each colleague and team member? If not, reflect on what these seemingly inconsequential team members bring that is of value to the team and organization. Ask others what they appreciate about each team member and listen well when they speak of those you minimize.

3. Do you need someone who can hold you accountable to the effective expression of your strength? Who might that be and what specifically would you ask them to contribute?

Chapter 2

Secure leaders pursue humility
and enjoy its freedoms.

Humility's Freedoms

On April 25, 2013, at the dedication of his presidential library, George W. Bush made repeated references to freedom and said: "I believe that freedom is a gift from God and the hope of every human heart." While Bush remains a polarizing figure, it is not difficult to believe that people yearn to be free. To be sure, there is externally imposed enslavement, but often the cruelest forms of imprisonment are self-imposed. We become our own worst masters as we shackle ourselves with pride. That's why humility should be so appealing - because it liberates. Let's explore three freedoms associated with humility.

#1: Freedom to learn

When I am humble, I recognize that I am not self-sufficient, never complete in myself, and certainly lacking the omniscience of our Creator. Not only am I not required to know everything, but I am free to experience the joy of continuous learning. More often than I wish to admit, I have fallen into the trap of saying I understand something when I clearly don't. Sometimes I only think I know something, sometimes I just don't want to listen to a long explanation about a subject of little interest, and then there are those times I am too embarrassed to admit my ignorance. Often, I am spared the further embarrassment of being called out - of having someone demand that I demonstrate my comprehension. If I am called out I may even choose to talk as if I do know something and hope that if I say enough words, I can overwhelm the listener into thinking that I know what I'm talking about. But there is no shame in saying, "I don't know." Even if it is something you should know already, there's no benefit to lying. Either you risk exposure, or you continue in your ignorance. Humility frees us from self-deification and encourages others as they share what they know with us.

#2: Freedom to make mistakes

The façade of perfection is impossible to maintain. Even dictators surrounded by trembling sycophants cannot fend off all reasonable scrutiny. "Don't confront me with my failures, I had not forgotten them," sings Jackson Browne in *These Days*. There is no shame in making mistakes, only in failing to grow and mature. One story I regularly share is that I had earned my PhD and was employed as a college professor before I found out that Rhode Island isn't actually an island. Worse (if that's possible), I found out from my students while teaching a course. Humility is not found in the mistake, but in how it is taken up into one's life and history. So, if you won't confront me, I'll confront myself with my failures because they remind me that I make mistakes and that's OK. I've been freed from the prison of self-deceptive perfection. In my humanity, I encourage others that they are free to be human as well.

#3: Freedom to need others

Vision/Alignment/Execution - these are the work of leaders. What I've discovered is that leaders typically excel at two of these three. I've never yet met the leader who excels at all three. Everyone needs the strengths of others and it is freeing to come to that realization. Our home is under renovation and numerous times during this process I have marveled at little things our contractor thinks to do that would never dawn on me until it was far too late. More than once I've said to him as he prepares to leave for the day: "I hope you're proud of what you've accomplished today. It's amazing what you're able to do." Humility releases me from solitary confinement and allows others to experience the joy of blessing me through the expression of their strengths and gifts.

Caveat

The freedom of humility is not realized in insecurity, weakness, lack of effort, or incompetence. False humility's attempts to trap others into praising us produces, at best, a momentary sugar high that leaves us feeling even more depleted when it wears off. It's not lasting, and it does not bring the freedom associated with a true attitude of humility. Humility is the path to freedom and its rewards are sweet, to be savored in our lives and in the lives of those with whom we interact.

Questions to consider:

1. In what areas of your life do you need to adopt an attitude of humility?

2. How would your organization change if humility were highly valued, beginning with leadership? What freedoms might you experience both personally and professionally if this were to occur?

3. Which freedom is most meaningful to you at this stage of your journey? Which should you begin pursuing and how will you do that?

Chapter 3

Regret-proof your life through consistent appraisal.

An Antidote to Regret

"When one door closes, another opens, but we often look so long and so regretfully upon the closed door that we do not see the one which has opened for us." – Alexander Graham Bell

Amazon.com was launched by founder Jeff Bezos in 1994. But to launch Amazon, Bezos had to abandon his career path to risk everything on a crazy idea. In making this decision, he applied his "regret minimization framework." This construct exists to reduce the regret he might otherwise feel for missing out on a fantastic opportunity. "Okay, now I'm looking back on my life. I want to have minimized the number of regrets I have. I knew that when I was 80 I was not going to regret having tried this. I was not going to regret trying to participate in this thing called the Internet that I thought was going to be a really big deal. I knew that if I failed, I wouldn't regret that, but I knew the one thing I might regret is not ever having tried. I knew that that would haunt me every day, and so, when I thought about it that way it was an incredibly easy decision." I'm pretty sure he made the right decision.

Few of us are going to abandon our current paths to risk everything on an entrepreneurial dream. We're more likely to tweak our direction by a few degrees. Even with this more cautious approach, we should aim to minimize regret. No one is perfect. While many preach the value of failure and making mistakes, clearly you shouldn't actively pursue them. You're going to make mistakes - the question is whether you learn from them. Asked another way, are you using your experience to gain an advantage? Periodically you should take time to ask yourself the following four questions about your work and calling - to assess your professional and personal success.

#1: What is working well?

These are places where often it is wise to invest additional time and resources. Exploit what's working until that well is a steady stream of productivity and success. There will always be more than enough ways to spend your time and resources. My clients are bombarded with ideas for growing their businesses - their problem isn't ideas. The challenge is sifting through those ideas to find the ones worth pursuing. If you've found something that's working, make sure you carefully assess all possible outcomes before you abandon it for the unproven promise of something better. Few ideas become Amazon.com.

#2: Is there another source you should be tapping?

This is an opportunity and a trap. An opportunity if you

can fully test and ramp up a new source alongside what is currently working. It's a trap if it causes you to abandon what is working to gamble on the unknown and that unknown comes up empty. This is the middle ground for the "have your cake and eat it too" crowd. We all know that the answer to that statement is most often "no, you can't," so be careful and don't get greedy. Of course, if your work is already failing, then a total overhaul may be your best hope.

#3: What hasn't been working?

Either revise or drop what isn't working. Revise if it is an issue of proper implementation, additional training, or some other reasonable tweak. Drop if it is a distraction from your core focus, it isn't practical given who you are, or it was a great theory that doesn't translate well into practice. This is the time to be ruthless in your assessment of whether something is working. This may be even more difficult if what you're considering dropping was your idea. Consider enlisting the support of others, given how difficult it is abandoning the ideas to which one has given birth.

#4: Will this work for me?

You are not going to change fundamentally who you are over the course of your life. What you can and should do is to become a mature version of yourself, building on your strengths and gifting, and surrounding yourselves with those who complement your areas of weakness. In the opening to the story of David and Goliath, David is offered the armor of King Saul to wear in his upcoming battle. David is a teenager who is much smaller than Saul and so Saul's armor only hinders his movement. Just because Saul's armor works for him does not mean it will work for you.

Bottom Line: Read all the books, listen to all the speakers, and then remember that what you are really hearing is someone saying, "This is what worked for me and I think you should try it" or even "This is an idea I had that I think sounds really good and is appealing to my audiences, I think you should try it" or finally, "This is an idea that is making me a lot of money, I hope you'll try it." Saul's armor may be a perfect fit, or it may simply weigh you down.

Questions to consider:

1. Do you have a "regret minimization framework"? Can you think of a specific example where you wish you had applied this strategy?

2. How are you demonstrating your commitment to realistically evaluating what is and is not working within your organization?

3. Is there some area of life or career that you need to shake up and change? What's holding you back? Who could provide wise counsel in making this change?

Chapter 4

*What pearls of wisdom have been
given to you and which
are you leaving for others?*

An Estate of Pearls

As I reflect on my time in the consulting business, I think about those who have made possible our success. My wife and business partner, Judy, was the one who told me to follow my dreams, even when she knew that dreams not yet realized cannot pay very real bills found in our mailbox. My father's words ring loudly through my life and influence all that I share. So, I want to share nine pearls of wisdom from my father.

1) When you make a decision, it becomes the right decision.

This doesn't mean that you cannot make mistakes or that there is never a need to retrace one steps to find the better path. It does mean that reflexive second-guessing is unproductive. Take risks. Commit to your decisions and, unless there is a clear reason to do otherwise, press forward. So, when you leave your job of 13 years and find yourself bringing in a grand total of $500 for a month's efforts, while surrounded by the greatest economic crisis since the Great Depression, don't turn back. Work hard, stay focused, and persevere.

2) If you read a book and get one good thing, it was worth reading.

Have you ever finished reading a book and thought to yourself, "Did it really have to be that long?" Or perhaps gotten part way through an article and simply lost focus? Even the Bible has passages that require discipline to plow through. This principle has helped me to appreciate books that I otherwise would have dismissed and has freed me as a facilitator to set a realistic bar for my sessions to meet. I tell participants, "If you get one thing from today's session, and that one thing may come from your colleagues or from within your thoughts, then it was worth your being here."

3) Each of us is here to serve people.

Every job involves serving others - directly or indirectly. We should celebrate every day we have the opportunity to serve others. Today I had a client who apologized to me for taking so much of my time and I told him: "I'm here to serve you. No worries." Serving others frees me from focusing on myself and allows me to find success in the success of others.

4) Live out your convictions without feeling the need to impose them on others.

Dad was a minister for 50 years. He had strong convictions about the connection between his faith and his behavior. As members of his family, we lived under the influence of those convictions. But to members of his congregation he always gave the freedom to develop their own convictions, even ones quite divergent from his own. Our job is not to convince others that we are right (although that is part of influencing others at times). Our job is to help others find what they are called to do. We are not here to impose our convictions on others, but to help them live out the convictions they have chosen to adopt.

5) Ask others for what you need but allow them the freedom to make a genuine decision.

"A 'no' is as good as a 'yes'." My dad often begins requests with this statement, a reminder to him and his listener that this request is an opportunity for the other to act freely. I tell my clients that I do not have an agenda for them (another favorite phrase of my father). I am there to help them reach a decision, but I'm the one who leaves, and they are the ones who stay to live with the decision. To be effective, decisions must be owned, and this will only happen when the decision is theirs to make.

6) We overestimate what we can accomplish in one year and underestimate what we can accomplish in five.

I had a seminar participant tell me that this phrase didn't originate with my father. I'm sure that's true. There are variants of this phrase attributed to a range of famous individuals. The point remains: It is my father's voice in which I hear this reminder that we need to take a longer view. I talk a lot about trajectory, about the direction of one's life, and this statement is one source of that focus. When we focus solely on the present and the short-term, time will always be fleeting and the to-do list far too long. This, in turn, becomes a cycle that will eventually prevent us from reaching our longer-term goals in life. Only when we take a longer view will we be able to work backwards in a way that allows us to balance the needs of today with the dreams of tomorrow. By the way, my father's view of today was captured by a theological insight: "There is enough time in each day to do God's will."

7) Pursue your calling and you'll find a way to pay the bills.

My father has always been agnostic toward money. Significantly, he told us that he never asked about his salary before accepting a job. While I am wired a bit differently on this subject, his recognition that money may be important, but it isn't a pursuit worthy of a human life, has influenced my desire to build reduced-fee and no-fee work for select not-for-profit clients into my business. I earned an undergraduate degree in philosophy - an employment dead end if ever there was one. Somehow that decision has led me to a place where I am living my dream, doing what I love, and having greater success (in many senses of that word) than I ever thought possible.

8) See the good in people without pretending that evil does not exist.

This insight took so many forms: A strong belief that people can be transformed both over time and in dramatic forward leaps, even when backsliding occurs; a commitment to long-term relationships that bear fruit in the lives of all involved, even when rocky at times; and an appreciation for those who share foundational commitments - my father would lead our Christmas Eve service and then attend midnight mass at a local Catholic church. I love my clients, meaning that I desire their best and work with them to realize the good, all the while recognizing that each of us is fallible (human) and prone to deviate from what is good.

9) Hard work is good.

We were taught to do more than was asked. If you were mowing a neighbor's lawn, then you trimmed as well. My dad used to say (or at least this is how I remember it): "If you want to be seen as a professional within the community while doing very little, then be a pastor." I never heard this as disparaging his own calling, but as a reminder that one reason many pastors never saw their congregations grow was that they failed to leave their offices to work among the people of their community. My dad visited his parishioners' homes, their workplaces, and ministered to them in the hospital. He worked hard to impact the lives of those in his care (including their family members, neighbors, and co-workers). "Hard work pays off" is not merely a familiar saying, but the result of continuous effort over time that is measured in many ways.

I am fully convinced that my father's estate will not be measured in dollars, but in pearls made available to invest in the development of our lives and character.

Questions to consider:

1. Which "pearl" resonates most with you? Why?

2. In what area of your life should you invest one of the "pearls"? How will you do this and how will you measure its impact?

3. Are there other "pearls" that have been passed down to you that you find worth sharing? Share one with a colleague or family member today.

Chapter 5

If you lose the value of your name,
what do you have left?

Protecting the Value of Your Name

"A good name is to be chosen rather than great riches, and favor is better than silver or gold." -- Proverbs 22:1, ESV

People focus effort on achieving many different things: An impressive career, a great looking family, a large bank balance, or a good name. To be recognized as a person of integrity requires us to consider the ways in which integrity can be expressed or squandered.

Integrity of resources - time and money

"Time is money." Familiar expressions are not always true. While time and money often intersect, they remain two distinct resources for us to invest.

Integrity of time involves giving people what they've paid for and not wasting what they've made available to you. I've had many jobs through the years, but one of the most challenging was cleaning houses while I was in graduate school. The challenge wasn't bending down to scrub a bathtub or moving all the knick-knacks to dust, it was the way the business was run. Clients paid by the hour and often my team was in and out of a house in 15-20 minutes when a homeowner had paid for an hour's worth of work. I wasn't in charge, but I was an employee representing a company that had no integrity with time. I'll never go there again. Making more money isn't worth sacrificing my name. That's why it's better (when possible) to charge for the work you do and the results you generate rather than for the time you spend.

Integrity of money extends into many areas. I'll mention two. I have an accountant who files my taxes each year and, while I tell others I wish he were more creative in finding deductions, I'm thankful that he takes a conservative approach that safeguards my integrity and makes me less liable to audit woes. Second, I was at our favorite pizza shop recently picking up my kids' favorite pizza when I noticed a new punch card they are giving out. Ten pickup orders entitle you to a free pizza. I asked them to punch the card for me and was told they don't have a hole punch, so the manager just put an "X" over the number 1. I asked what would keep someone from going home and putting an "X" over the other nine numbers, thus getting a free pizza. He said, "I guess nothing." I told him, "Just so you know, my integrity is worth more to me than a free pizza."

Integrity of character - behavior and speech

Some people want to separate words from actions, but

clearly words are actions*. That's why they have such impact on our lives. I'm willing to bet each of you can remember a specific hurtful comment that was made to you. "Sticks and stones may break my bones, words may just destroy me."

What frustrates people is when our words and actions don't line up. When we speak and don't follow through. For example, dreamers get excited about an idea or project, but their enthusiasm may not translate into the behavior needed to make it real. That may be OK when people know how to interpret what you say but can lead to confusion among team members when you're in charge. Here are three principles for leaders to keep in mind:

1. When communicating with idea generators, ask: "Did we reach a decision or were we just talking?" Idea generators may be surprised to realize you were taking marching orders from something they were simply musing about.

2. The advice of Jesus is something I work to follow: "Let your 'yes' be 'yes' and your 'no' be 'no.'" Most commentators interpret Jesus' words as an admonition to avoid the unnecessary layers of promises and vows, just be a person of your word. Say what you mean.

3. Avoid hypocrisy and a lifestyle that says, "Do as I say and

not as I do." Make sure you don't ask others to be better than you are willing to be or to go where you're unwilling to go.

Integrity isn't a sexy topic, but an honored name is your most important possession. It is difficult to earn over a long period of time; easy to lose in a moment; nearly impossible to rebuild.

[*Note: See "Words ARE Action" for more on this topic.]

Questions to consider:

1. How good is your word? Does your organization reflect the value that you place on integrity? Are you satisfied with this?

2. Does your organization, and you as a leader, have a good name? What are you doing to protect this?

3. Time, money, behavior and speech – which area gives you the biggest struggle? What needs to change?

Section 2

The Leader's Role: Crafting Vision

One of the three core activities of leadership is crafting vision. Vision is the oxygen that enables organizations to continue living and growing. It is the awareness of the big picture, the long-term, and the overall objectives. It describes a desirable future for the organization, those it employs, and those it serves.

Leaders are responsible for there being organizational vision even if they are not themselves the crafters of those visions. They must make sure that the vision is seen, communicated, and understood. From there they build alignment around that vision and drive the execution of it, but those are activities for later sections of this book.

"Creating a Shared Cultural Language" emphasizes the need for a common language through which the vision can be expressed.

"*What Leaders See*" takes the metaphor of vision and identifies key elements that should be part of each leader's vision.

"*Always Have a Good Story to Tell*" looks at the power of storytelling and the need for positive stories that attract stakeholders to the shared vision.

"*Control Your Focus*" reminds leaders that vision can be distracted and misdirected; one must discipline oneself to focus on those elements that contribute to the vision.

"*The Maturing Organization*" examines how organizations evolve over time and the relationship of maturity to organizational vision.

Find your role in crafting vision and make sure that your organization never lacks the oxygen it needs to thrive.

Chapter 6

Words matter, choose wisely.

Creating a Shared Cultural Language

Successful organizations create definable cultures built upon words and phrases that are known, understood, and used consistently. At its heart, culture in this sense can be defined as shared knowledge. This refers to all the things people need to know within your organization to do their jobs correctly and efficiently. It's also what makes your organization stand out from the crowd; it's what's unique; it's what sets you apart from the rest. I use Everything DiSC and Five Behaviors of a Cohesive Team to enable my clients to talk about personality styles, communication preferences, and team health in a consistent and productive manner. These tools create a common language to build upon - one that each team member can understand and use consistently. Apart from adopting a pre-constructed language such as DiSC, what are the steps to creating a shared cultural language?

[An early reader of this book made the following observation with which we agree. We'll allow Mark Pontious to speak for himself, when he says: *"The only comment I have on this section (which I love, overall) is that this may seem too abstract for someone who isn't at the top levels of an organization, but more of a department head, etc. I could see someone saying 'But I don't have influence of the vision of my entire organization and we already have those values and phrases at the organizational level. Who am I to create new ones?' I assume you would reply to that person that their unit within the organization can/should have their own values and phrases that align with the larger vision of the whole organization."]*

#1: Keep an idea file

I encourage leaders to start by keeping a file containing all their principles, professional insights, and commonly used phrases (whether those phrases are original, stolen, or stolen and so deeply embedded over time that they feel original). From this file, they can begin the process of intentionally creating a cultural language. I am talking about a literal file here where things are written down and observable. Whether in an online document or a handwritten journal, get these ideas in writing.

#2: Commit to specific words and phrases

Commit to ways of saying things so that they become memorable touch-points for team members. So, for example, when I talked with a client about hiring and said, "You need to guard your front door so that you don't have to use your back door as often," this resonated. When they are looking to add team members they talk about "guarding the front door." They could talk about hiring well and generally accepted principles that make success more likely, but the image of guarding a door has greater impact and is memorable shorthand for what they are seeking to accomplish. Thus, this phrase, over time, becomes a shared piece of language that everyone in the hiring process uses regularly.

#3: Be consistent in your use of cultural words and phrases

Don't allow people to use key terms in ways that are inconsistent with culture. If you have decided that "leading is a one-to-many relationship" while "managing is a one-to-one relationship," then make sure that "leading" and "managing" are kept separate and used consistently. If words are left unintentionally ambiguous or vague, their power will be diminished. This can be a challenge as popular buzz words have a way of popping up, infiltrating the organization, and then getting used so frequently that they burn out and lose their meaning. You want your words and phrases to last, so choose wisely not only the "what" but also the "when" and "where" of your language.

#4: Correct team members' word choices as needed

You must be intentional in guiding people to use this common language. One of my clients insists that team members refer to their clients as clients of the team and not as clients of an individual team member. No one on that team has his or her own clients. Clients are associated with the team as a whole and this is a central part of the culture that has been crafted. Remember, you are creating culture around a shared language. Be intentional about your choice of words and phrases as well as being clear about what those words and phrases represent. Be consistent in your usage. Correct one another as needed.

#5: WARNING: Abstract idea alert - The use of enthymemes

Team members will begin to hear these words and phrases in their heads and will complete your argument in support of culture even when you aren't around to influence them directly. This may sound a lot like the parenting process. That's not by mistake. In rhetoric, there is a type of argument called an enthymeme where the speaker does not spell out each element of his argument but allows the audience members to supply a portion of the argument from their shared belief system. This engages the minds of the audience members directly and results in a level of self-persuasion that is deeper than simply hearing a speaker lay out his case. Create cultural enthymemes.

Questions to consider:

1. Does your organization have a definable culture? What is it?

2. What are the words and phrases that are significant to your organization?

3. Do you think your organization could benefit from creating cultural enthymemes? How could you go about doing this? (You might want to Google "enthymeme".)

Chapter 7

A leader's vision gives sight to others.

What Leaders See

"If you are working on something exciting that you really care about, you don't have to be pushed. The vision pulls you." – Steve Jobs

There are no great leaders, living or dead, who lack great vision. Whether at the ballot box or on the battlefield, inside the boardroom or on the athletic court, focusing on organization or family, great leaders leverage vision to create forward movement. Vision is the foundational element that pulls a company into success and starts at the top. A leader lacking vision will cause an organization to stagnate and wither.

Here are four characteristics of great vision.

#1: Focus on elements at more than one depth

A few summers ago, our family took a trip out west. We spent miles driving through walls of trees, as well as expanses so open that if the earth were flat you could have seen to the edge. Neither extreme was the most interesting or made for great pictures. Any good photographer knows that great views have a large depth of field with objects at varying depths. Your eye is drawn to the various elements that stand out from and complement one another.

<u>Visionary leaders</u> focus on elements at more than one depth and interpret what they see for themselves and others. They need to see clearly what is near, at the midpoint, and far away. This can be interpreted temporally - seeing today, this year, and into the future. It can also be interpreted organizationally - seeing the current organization, its emerging structure, and the can-only-be-imagined form of the future.

#2: See emerging beauty in the yet-to-be realized

The best views are those unspoiled by man or nature - where beauty appears untainted. But sometimes there is emerging beauty that is hidden to most. The Crazy Horse monument in South Dakota is so far from completion that it didn't immediately capture my imagination - especially when one has just visited the iconic Mount Rushmore. However, once you see the informational film on Crazy Horse explaining the project, its origin, and its eventual objective, you can begin to see the emerging beauty in an unfinished sculpture protruding from the side of a mountain. You see the Native American chief astride his horse, pointing to his lands.

<u>Inspiring leaders</u> don't allow challenging circumstances, ready-at-hand excuses, or the attitudes of others to keep them from seeing the beauty around them. More than that, they inspire others to see emerging beauty in the yet-to-be realized.

#3: See the connection to people

Some vistas should make for beautiful pictures but lose their meaning when they are disassociated from the people who experienced them together. Have you ever been coerced into looking at an endless array of photos on someone's phone (or, in my day, a slide show), only to think to yourself that you would rather be anywhere, doing anything else? It's people that give meaning to the world around them. Endless photos of landscapes, no matter how gorgeous, get old fast. That's why we kept encouraging (read "coercing") our children to step into our pictures. Yet even with people in the pictures, if you weren't there for the experience, most of the meaning will still be lost. Have you ever shown someone a picture that moved you with the associated memories, only to receive a noncommittal response? That's when you realize: "I guess you had to be there."

<u>Transformational leaders</u> know that calling gains meaning as it serves and impacts people. Beauty really is in the eye of the beholder and great leaders know how to attract eyes, move

hearts, and influence minds so that the people of an organization are transformed through the connection of their work to the lives of others. Their influence transports you where you need to be to appreciate their vision.

#4: Be drawn to the personally compelling

It never ceases to amaze me how different people are from one another. My daughter's favorite part of the trip was San Francisco. My wife's was Yellowstone. Mine were those moments when I saw unfiltered joy on the faces of my family members - when even the most cynical teenager couldn't keep delight from seeping forth.

Reproducing leaders find their calling compelling. They believe in something because it stirs them - perhaps in ways that few others are stirred. Along the way they attract others to their calling and release new leaders to carry on the vision.

This picture from our trip captures all four elements:

1. There are objects at varying depths that attract your attention.

2. There is emerging beauty in a dry landscape waiting for seasonal rains and in a shoe tree that continues to evolve.

3. There is a connection to people - one shoe was inscribed: "To my friends from Ohio."

4. I found it compelling - our youngest alerted us to it after we had passed it by. We were a few miles from our destination for the day and I just wanted to be done driving, but something in his voice told me that he thought he had seen something special and that drew me (uncharacteristically) to retrace our path so we could see it. It was a moment of shared joy - which was the real reason for our trip. A reminder that unplanned moments on the journey may be more significant than the anticipated destination.

Questions to consider:

1. In what area(s) of your life are you working on something that excites you and pulls you toward completion?

2. Are you a leader of great vision? Which of the four characteristics described above is most compelling for you?

3. What type of leadership (visionary, inspiring, transformational, reproducing) is your strength? Are there other types you would like to develop? If so, what will you do to add them to your repertoire?

Chapter 8

Storytelling is an essential leadership skill, but it's not storytelling if no one's listening.

Always Have a Good Story to Tell!

"The most powerful person in the world is the storyteller. The storyteller sets the vision, values, and agenda of an entire generation that is to come." — Steve Jobs

When I started my business, I quickly learned that no one wanted to hear how things were **really** going - at least very few. Besides, who would hire the struggling consultant? So, I learned that the answer to "How are you doing?" was always "Great!" accompanied by a positive story. This wasn't deceptive but was based on the realization that there was always a good story worth telling.

One of my clients recently quoted a team member as saying: "If I've told you this story before, don't stop me; I want to hear it again!" What are the stories from your professional or personal life that you love to hear repeated? Are they stories that celebrate your success or ones that showcase others in a starring role?

There can be power in self-deprecating humor - to a point. Remember my story from Chapter 2 of how after earning a PhD from Northwestern University, I found out, to my amazement, that Rhode Island isn't an island? The point of the story is that no one knows everything and we all get embarrassed at times, so we need to learn to laugh at ourselves.

I've had the privilege of serving teams in several African countries and have shared with some of my clients and friends the story of how I passed out in the Tunis Airport. While that event was not the highlight of my trip, the gracious responses of the people around me and my first experience of moving through an airport in a wheelchair make for a memorable story.

Some of the benefits of stories:

- Stories draw people in and build connection.

- Stories reveal elements about you that may be of value to others - often in ways that are more interesting, memorable, and attractive than making the point directly.

- Stories can be told to relay facts or to make a point. I tell stories to make a point which may make them more interesting, but likely a bit less accurate.

- Stories need to be relevant to the larger point you are making - they should not overshadow your primary communication purpose (like a great introduction to a speech that goes downhill from there).

- Stories are memorable - think of the parables of Jesus and the longevity they enjoy.

Here are some ideas for the use of stories within your team:

- Everyone is in sales and each team member should have a positive story to share with those who have interest in your organization.

- Sharing stories is a great way to celebrate your team and team members' success.

- Use stories to convey lasting principles that you want team members to remember.

- Consider whether you are telling a story to convey facts or to make a point and tailor what you include to fit your objective.

Remember: Not all stories that interest you are of interest to others. Watch for signs that people are tuning you out. This is where sales advice I received comes into play: "Be curious, not interesting." People want to talk about themselves. So, if you ask questions and listen well, you will be more attractive and more likely to make the sale. Of course, you may be lonely at times when others don't reciprocate.

Always have a good story to tell, while remembering that allowing others to tell their stories may be of a greater value to what you are seeking to accomplish. "If I've told you this story before, don't stop me; I want to hear it again!" is both humorous and ineffective.

Questions to consider:

1. What is your favorite story to tell? What is it about this story that drives you to repeat it?

2. How could effective storytelling be better utilized within your organization?

3. "Be curious, not interesting." How can you put this advice into practice for yourself and among those you lead?

Chapter 9

Your focus as a leader determines what your organization sees.

Control Your Focus!

Which of these pyramids would you rather visit? I've visited both. In college, I took a trip to Israel, Jordan, and Egypt, and there I met my wife, but that's another story. The pictures above are of the same pyramids - the Pyramids of Giza, just outside of Cairo. Viewed from the desert they appear isolated and imposing. Viewed from Cairo they are still awe-inspiring, but often obscured by smog.

Our lives as leaders are often like these pictures of the pyramids. Viewed from one direction they are rewarding and significant. Viewed from another they are unclear and uninspiring. Don't let the promotional brochures for the pyramids of others' lives blind you to the fact that every leader's world has days with smog, congested traffic, crumbling infrastructure, and overcrowding. Those are days we long for clarity, smooth passage, stability, and solitude. Like Superman, we need our Fortress of Solitude where we can retreat for insight and inspiration. It's all a matter of perspective. What is real may be expressed in different ways, each of which is true. If the glass is half empty, then it is half full. This is where leaders must influence others to see a perspective, knowing they will be accused by half-emptiers of only imagining the glass to be half-full. Why is this important? Because the perspective that you choose will frame the reality and vision of your organization.

To keep perspective, here are five principles related to our focus as leaders.

#1: Focus on the appropriate level (it's not the weeds).

If you are a leader, then focus on the development and utilization of your key subordinates. Stories from the front line may be important to your understanding of the organization, but if you get into the weeds, then all you will see are weeds. Allow each of your gardeners to oversee his portion of the farm, tending its plants, removing the weeds, and managing the soil. If you want to focus your time on growing tomatoes, then you shouldn't be the one overseeing the farm.

#2: Focus on what is rather than what might have been.

Be a realist - there will be weeds. Look at your garden with unclouded vision. Don't get sucked into the never-ending game of "what might have been" rather than focusing on what is. The Giza pyramids without Cairo may be enticing, but don't bode well for tourism and commerce. There are reasons Cairo and the pyramids are in proximity to one another. Pesticide may remove all weeds from your garden, but too much pesticide will render your soil unusable. Your gardeners must keep doing the difficult work of weeding, so that you can focus on your farm growing what it exists to produce.

#3: Focus on trend lines rather than snapshots.

It is too easy to make it all about today. If it is smoggy and congested, then deal with the underlying issues rather than being paralyzed by the realization that your organization isn't perfect. Healthy organizations aren't perfect, they are headed in the right direction and know what is contributing to their success and what is continuing to hold them back. In life, we don't arrive, we move toward the realization of meaningful goals. Don't let today's variable conditions distract from the longer view.

#4: Focus on strengths without ignoring the weaknesses that will bring you to your knees.

I worked for an organization that spent its deferred maintenance dollars on daily operations. Over a period of years, the buildings began to deteriorate and the price to repair them was soon unimaginably large. That is, until a new treasurer arrived who stopped the practice of robbing tomorrow's funds for today's bills and began reversing that trend. It was a lengthy process, but ultimately achievable once tackled in a systematic and disciplined fashion. Weeds kill - healthy organizations don't ignore entrenched weeds because they appear to have roots that have grown too deep, they dig deep and remove them.

#5: Focus on people and not on things.

Life is about people. Each of us exists to serve others through our strengths and callings. When you focus on things, you confuse the means with the ends. I tell people I want a maintenance free home. But a home is for people and as long as there are people, walls will be scuffed, furniture will be scratched, windows will grow dirty, and carpets will need to be cleaned. Minimizing damage is commendable, but not if it requires driving the people from the home. An abandoned home soon will be beyond repair and in need of razing. Gardens exist to feed people. People do not exist to serve gardens. Always maintain clarity on this distinction.

Questions to consider:

1. Which pyramid would you rather visit? Why? What do you do when you realize that both pyramids are the same?

2. Does your perspective tend to focus on the half-empty or half-full? How does this impact you and those you influence?

3. What areas of your garden need attention? Is this work that should be done by you or by others?

Chapter 10

Aging is inevitable;
maturity is a choice.

The Maturing Organization

As a parent, I've bristled at the notion of "raising children." In my mind, this phrase provokes an image of a 30-year-old child still living at home with no job, no friends, and nowhere to go but my basement. I prefer the expression "raising adults." In many respects, one of my primary jobs as a parent is to raise this person up to be an upstanding, positively contributing member of society; in other words, a mature adult. In the same vein, an organization that doesn't take seriously the need to grow into maturity is going to be left with an underdeveloped and immature core. Immaturity is not a recipe for long-term success and profitability. Where are you and your organization on the path to organizational maturity? What steps do you need to take to encourage this maturation?

Having worked for and with a wide range of organizations, I've come to recognize three stages in organizational development and some of the opportunities and challenges associated with each.

Phase I: Getting Started

The startup phase of an organization can be both challenging and fun. Typically, the team meets around a table to discuss all items of importance and reaches decisions by consensus. Often this is a positive period relationally, but decision-making can be slowed by the feeling that everyone needs to be present to discuss and make decisions. Because startups may attract generalists and entrepreneurial types who enjoy having influence, team members grow accustomed to speaking into all corners of the organization, including those that are outside their areas of expertise and responsibility. This can feel like a highly unified period of development.

Phase II: Growing Complexity

As the organization grows, the leaders no longer fit around the table. It is counterproductive to have all of them discussing each significant decision, since many decisions are not relevant to their areas of expertise or responsibility. Leaders experience a great deal of autonomy and operate freely within their silos. As long as the individual silos are successful, it feels as though the organization is successful. Relationships among leaders may begin to suffer or be non-existent as people are added to the organization. Neither decisions nor decision-making processes are consistent across silos and the silos often must compete for limited resources, sometimes focusing on individual success rather than on team or organizational success. Unfortunately, this is as far as some organizations come.

Phase III: Reaching Maturity

Hopefully, the organization recognizes the need to enter the mature phase of organizational development. The senior leaders develop and implement a unified vision that drives activity within and across the silos. They don't view silos as evil - they often allow areas of the organization to work efficiently, focusing on their competencies and responsibilities. At the same time, the organization recognizes the need for standardized policies and procedures. While leaders across the organization may affirm this need, they will often act as though they are the exceptions or explicitly seek to be the exceptions to these newly implemented policies and procedures. Behaviorally and emotionally, leaders resist the loss of autonomy and freedom while intellectually acknowledging the need for change. The organization must work to keep "corporate" from being interpreted as "evil empire." This stage can lead to unified success where the success of individual silos is insufficient and where rewards are tied to both individual and organizational performance. No longer are roles and responsibilities tied to particular individuals. Instead, the organization distinguishes between positions and personnel and creates roles and responsibilities based on position. Team members recognize that positions are held at this point in time by these individuals and are encouraged to shed the confusion that individuals own the positions they hold. Ultimately, silos must remember that they are not the farm, but exist to support the success of the farm.

Caveat

Leaders must choose to undertake this organizational journey. Children inevitably become adults, but maturity is not guaranteed. Similarly, movement from Phase I to Phase II can happen to an organization, but movement to and maintenance of Phase III must be intentional and ongoing. Along the way, leaders must relinquish the opportunity to speak into all areas of the organization and must surrender some autonomy to foster a healthy community that impacts more people than Phase I or Phase II ever allow. The maturity phase, if not managed intentionally, can lead to increasingly fractured leadership as some struggle to relinquish their perceived power and influence. This fracturing, at best, may drag the organization back into a Phase II level of functioning. At worst, it could spell disaster for the organization and lead to a complete reboot to Phase I.

Questions to consider:

1. Where would you place your organization along this three-phase continuum? Are you satisfied with this placement? How will you maintain your Phase III maturity or continue to move in that direction?

2. Where do you see the tension between the need for organizational structure and the resulting loss of autonomy by individual leaders or silos? What can be done to better manage this tension?

3. How do you need to develop and what changes do you need to make to better position yourself to lead a Phase III organization?

Section 3

The Leader's Role: Building Alignment

After crafting vision, leaders must build alignment around those visions. Many strong leaders stumble at this point. They see the future and understand what must be done to get there. They simply find it a distraction and a waste of time trying to get people on board the train. They have told people what must happen and why, and they expect reasonable people to reach the obvious conclusion - "I must pursue the vision as outlined by the leader."

Most people, however, are not logic-driven. Passions, interests, relationships, personal objectives all compete for attention and modify the "obvious conclusion" so that people do not pursue the vision with the commitment that the leader assumed would naturally arise. Leaders must slow down and build alignment around the vision if the execution of behaviors that will bring the vision to reality is to occur.

"You're Playing Junior High for Money" discusses the ways alignment is derailed by the immaturity of organizational members.

"A Grown Man Should Close the Fridge" addresses the opportunity for team members to take service to a level that few pursue; this is an indicator of alignment to the vision.

"Three Signs Your Team Is in Trouble - Deep Trouble!" looks at teams that are misaligned and the warning signs you should recognize.

"Lying Your Way to Peace" reminds leaders that deception is not a long-term leadership strategy, but eventually will drive people away from you and your vision.

"Zombie Horses Will Kill You" examines the need for clear expectations so that alignment is real and unthreatened by the zombie horses that otherwise may roam your halls.

Slow down to build alignment and your vision is more likely to be realized and to persist.

Chapter 11

As the leader, set the tone by communicating as an adult.

You're Playing Junior High for Money!

"Would I rather be feared or loved? Easy. Both. I want people to be afraid of how much they love me."
— Michael Scott of *The Office*

Building alignment within your team isn't possible when you're playing junior high for money (one thing Michael Scott embodied). What does "junior high for money" sound like? Well, have you ever heard an exchange like this among your colleagues?

"I knew she didn't like me."

"Why do you say that?"

"Because I heard that she told Tim that my idea for the product launch was risky and unworkable."

"Did you actually hear her say that?"

"Well, no, but I trust what Bruce tells me. I worked on the product launch for weeks and I don't appreciate her bad-mouthing my ideas to leadership."

We're back in junior high with its cliques, worries about social status, gossip and innuendo, and there's no end in sight. The only difference is that we're getting paid and some of the nerds have finally made good on their brainpower.

Much of my work is with successful organizations that are hindered by the emotional immaturity of team members. Experts in their fields, who offer quality services and products to their customers, they are subject to varying degrees of drama consistently undermining their team's cohesion and threatening its continued success.

What can be done to address these challenges?

#1: Make sure that expectations are clear and that team members are held consistently to these expectations.

Many organizations tire of repeating expectations and assume that new team members will pick them up from the culture that has been created. Stronger organizations commit resources to regularly communicating their expectations, even among team members who have heard them before. Then they hold team members accountable to these expectations, not allowing favoritism or fatigue to set in so that violations can slide unchallenged.

#2: Encourage team members to speak directly to one another, and do *not* allow yourself to be triangulated.

Triangulation occurs when you become the middleman between individuals or factions rather than pushing them back toward each other, insisting that they communicate with each other directly. At times it is appropriate to sit in as a third party, but you must do so as a fair-minded observer and not as an advocate for any of the entities involved.

#3: Persist in the eradication of poor behavior.

One conversation rarely solves a behavioral problem, particularly one that is recurring. You will have to have the conversation multiple times. What you are looking for is a decrease in the frequency and the intensity of these reminders. Eliminating a behavior takes time and repeated reminders. This feels like, and is, work. You can complain that you shouldn't have to do this, but avoiding this work will only encourage the behavior to continue and eventually you will be tempted to surrender the issue to the persistent offender.

#4: Recognize that personal security is foundational to healthy teams.

Unless team members are functionally secure, both

professionally and personally, they will not trust others and cannot be expected to handle constructive disagreement with maturity. You cannot make people secure, but you can contribute to that security with feedback that is behavioral, tied to your expectations, and expresses confidence that team members can continue to grow and mature.

#5: Bring in an outside expert to assist you in these efforts.

I don't anticipate being unemployed as long as driver-less cars don't lead to human-less teams. The need for people is every organization's greatest challenge, but it is also your greatest opportunity; the opportunity to tap into team members' creativity, empathy, productivity, and commitment to quality.

Personality assessments enable people to better understand themselves and to appreciate those around them, recognizing how differences complement varying strengths. Facilitators allow leaders to focus on what is happening among team members in a session rather than on delivering content. Even when a leader is a skilled presenter it is difficult to do both well - present and observe; deliver content and connect with your team members. We make it possible for you to focus where you will gain the greatest benefit - the observation of your team members interacting about meaningful topics.

Questions to consider:

1. Where does emotional immaturity lurk within your organization?

2. As a leader, do you consistently articulate and model adherence to clear expectations? Are your team members held accountable to these expectations?

3. What steps can be taken to grow the emotional maturity of your team members? How might an outside facilitator be of value in your attempted escape from junior high for money?

Chapter 12

*Serving others is an opportunity
to bless and be blessed.*

A Grown Man Should
Close the Fridge!

Alignment of a team to a vision can be undermined by a lack of respect for leadership from whom the vision flows. For example, what happens when a grown man can't close a refrigerator door or turn off the water? Someone has a decision to make.

For Rosanne Badowski, executive assistant to Jack Welch while CEO of GE, the answer was simple. You follow behind Welch and close the refrigerator or turn off the water. As the right-hand confidante to the CEO of an organization with more than 300,000 employees spread across the globe, Badowski knew that her role was to serve, and she embraced it with relish. The lessons from these experiences are recorded in her book, *Managing Up*.

I've identified what I call the AAAs of Service, three distinct levels available to all who serve.

Level #1: Accept assigned work.

This should be self-explanatory and is the point at which we begin teaching our children by assigning chores for them to complete. When we choose to serve, we must be willing to accept assigned work that is appropriate to our role, if it is not illegal, unethical, or demeaning. This requires humility of spirit and involves skills such as clarifying expectations and prioritizing activity. This is the ground floor of service and is often the minimal standard required for employment.

Level #2: Ask for additional work.

Once our children are employed outside the home, we teach them to never sit idle. If possible, they should seek additional work so that they remain busy. Those providing this second level of service are often considered to be "go-getters" or "overachievers." This level is typically a prerequisite to greater authority and responsibility associated with professional advancement. This level moves beyond fulfilling the minimal requirements to the expression of organizational commitment and a desire to develop one's capacity. Many people spend their entire careers at Levels #1 and #2.

Level #3: Anticipate the needs of those you serve (both internal and external clients).

A desire to exhibit Level #3 service is what motivated Badowski to follow Welch, closing the refrigerator and turning off the water, rather than growing angry with his neglect of basic life skills. She was proud to serve the CEO of, what was at that time, the nation's largest publicly traded company. In ways large and small, Badowski spent her career anticipating the needs of those she served. This is why Welch reached out to her when he left GE, asking her to continue as his assistant. This top-floor service is open to all who are capable of anticipating and meeting the needs of those they serve, but it remains largely unoccupied because its requirements are viewed by some as too demanding or possibly demeaning.

Level #3 is built upon three characteristics:

1. **Humility:** You must view service as a calling that capitalizes on your strengths and elevates your value to the organization.

2. **Belief:** You must believe in the mission of the organization within which you serve.

3. **Trust:** You must trust the leader you serve.

I get out of bed each day privileged to serve others in ways that draw upon my strengths and enhance their professional and personal success. I strive to provide Level #3 service. It allows me to maximize my influence and the utilization of my gifts and, to me, is in no way demeaning, but is an honor.

Questions to consider:

1. Do you see examples of Level #3 service within your team and organization? Are you modeling this behavior for others?

2. Does your organization consider Level #1 or #2 to be your minimal participation standard? Are your team members aware of this expectation?

3. If you struggle with Level #3 service, can it be traced to issues with humility, belief, or trust? If so, how can you address those concerns?

Chapter 13

Address team health before the illness is terminal.

Three Signs Your Team is in Trouble - Deep Trouble!

The evening news tells stories of elite teams with troubled players. How many times must we hear of highly paid athletes being arrested for drug possession or domestic violence? How many more will be suspended due to the use of steroids or other performance enhancing drugs? Even Little League coaches and parents get into all-out brawls at the neighborhood park. Unfortunately, the problems of individual team members spread to impact the entire team.

How do you know if your team is in trouble? Three sure signs provide evidence of failing health and lack of alignment.

Sign #1: Factions are forming

People disagree, and people grow annoyed with others. That leads them to vent about one another. So far, so normal. When venting turns into faction-forming, you've got a problem. What's the difference? Venting is letting off steam, expressing emotions, or explaining why you find someone else's behavior irritating. Faction-forming is when you recruit others to your cause and to your opposition to another team member. What started out as a few individuals with a gripe has morphed into a playground version of picking teams. Factions are deadly because a team becomes a collection of competing sub-teams who are no longer committed to one another's success or to communicating assertively (i.e., clearly and directly). In fact, if left unchecked, rival factions can even engage in sabotage to the detriment of the overall goals and purpose of the larger team. I refer to this as "junior high for money" - we are exhibiting the immature divisiveness of junior high while getting paid. (This was discussed in greater detail in chapter 11.)

Sign #2: Team members cheer for the failure of those on the same team

People disagree, and people grow annoyed with others. This leads them to oppose decisions associated with those they find annoying and encourages them to hope that the decisions fail, proving that the other is wrong. It doesn't matter whether the other person's ideas have merit or if the decision reached is clearly positive for the whole team. The negative association colors the view of anything coming from that source. There is a fine line between hoping that a person's idea will fail and working to that end. Once this line is crossed and team members are actively engaged in sabotaging internal efforts, there's little hope of success. If your competitors most effective weapons are members of your own team, you are in trouble -

deep trouble. In the words of Jesus: "A house divided against itself cannot stand."

Sign #3: There's an absence of conflict

Some signs of trouble are easily confused with signs of health. Weight loss, typically associated with healthy eating and regular exercise, can be a sign of cancer. Teams without visible disagreement may look peaceful, however, they may be suffering from a growth-deadening disease. Examples of such a disease include team members insufficiently engaged to speak up, group-think that eliminates originality, or apathy about making improvements. Put two people in a room and give them three topics to discuss. If they are being honest and seeking the best outcomes they will have different and even conflicting ideas. That's normal and healthy. Artificial harmony is appealing, but deadly. Healthy teams are made up of strong individuals who disagree, challenge one another's ideas, reach well-considered decisions, and then commit to those decisions even if they disagree. They may work to refine implementation and insist on rigorous evaluation, but they don't cheer for failure or slink away uncommitted.

So, what do you do if some (or all) of these symptoms are evident in your organization? Act. Don't wait for the illness to spread further – some illnesses are terminal and then no cure remains. Action may take the form of mediation if conflict is primarily among a small group of people. Reshuffling team members or responsibilities may help if more than a few have gotten dragged into the conflict and factions are forming. In extreme situations, you may need to disband the team and start over with a fresh set of people that aren't colored by the unhealthiness of the previous group. Bringing in a facilitator to observe and recommend solutions from an outside perspective is often beneficial. There's no quick cure when dealing with troubled teams but doing nothing will not lead to restored health.

Questions to consider:

1. Are your teams showing any signs of discontent or conflict? How would you know if they were? Is there a troubling absence of conflict? How should you respond?

2. What solutions have you used in the past to build team cohesiveness and address team conflict? Do you need to employ any of these strategies again?

3. Who can you enlist to help teams avoid this in the first place? Are you willing to look beyond your own strengths and engage others in this process?

Chapter 14

Build a long-term culture of healthy truth-telling, rather than settling for the short-term benefits of lies.

Lying your Way to Peace

You cannot lie your way to peace, even when speaking the truth seems just too difficult. I'm sure there are some readers whose immediate reaction is: "Of course you can lie your way to peace. I do it all the time." In fact, I know one person in my life who says "no" by saying "yes." He smiles and nods along with you, agreeing with what you say, and then promptly forgets or chooses to forget the conversation once you've left the room. Rather than taking you on directly and having to deal with the difficulty of saying "no," he just agrees and then ignores. My impression is that he never intended to do what he just agreed to and so I rarely interpret his enthusiastic support as being sincere. I also avoid interacting with him when possible.

What is a lie?

It is not merely saying something false, because I may say something false believing it to be true (I'm sitting in a room without windows and tell you it is raining because it was when I arrived five minutes ago, but now it is quite sunny). It may be saying something true, because I may say something true while believing it to be false (I tell you that I bought tickets to a charity event I don't want to attend, but about which I want you to quit bugging me, forgetting that in a moment of weakness months ago I actually did buy the tickets). Here's the bottom line, lying is communicating with the intention to deceive. So, whether what I say is true or false, if I intend to deceive you, I am lying.

Misunderstanding may look like lying

Using terminology from Myers-Briggs Type Indicator, those with an extroverting preference (E - they tend to think out loud), who also have a perceiving preference (P - they like to be spontaneous, flexible, and adaptable) are sometimes seen as deceptive or lying when they are not intending to deceive. What happens is that these EP's are out gathering information and they run into those having a judging preference (J - they like to be decisive, planned, and orderly). Js look to draw conclusions and decisions from conversation. So, the EP is gathering information and the J is looking to reach a decision. They both interpret the conversation from within their own framework. Eventually three Js meet up in the lunchroom and discuss what the EP has said. "Well he told me we are going to do X." "No, I spoke with him and he said we are going to do Y." "Well, that's odd. I distinctly heard him commit us to Z." What are these three people to conclude? As those with a judging preference, they conclude that the EP is dishonest and deceptive, that he only tells people what they want to hear, and that he commits to multiple paths to keep everyone happy while he ends up doing whatever he wants. In actuality, he committed to nothing, but was simply considering options. It is his enthusiasm that led the Js to hear commitment where there was none.

Five principles related to truth-telling:

1. Not all truth needs to be spoken. Sometimes it is simply best not to speak. It may be better to deflect a question with a question or to redirect attention elsewhere rather than always speaking truth.

2. Not all truth needs to be spoken now. Sometimes it is best to wait and see whether it will remain necessary for you to speak.

3. The truth needs to be spoken in love. How you say something is often just as important as what you say. You may need to speak truth on an uncomfortable issue, but if you can empathize with the recipient and see the world from her perspective, you may choose your words more carefully.

4. Your truth may not be the truth of others. Each of us sees the world from a perspective that is not the final, privileged view from which truth can be seen without distortion. None of us is God. This is not to say that there isn't genuine truth - just that you aren't the one person

best positioned to say in every instance what it must be.

5. Lying provides only short-term avoidance of truth. It often appears that lying is the best choice even if it isn't the best policy. But long-term truth has a way of emerging and lies tend to have a short shelf-life before they mold and decay. Besides, it takes a lot of effort to keep your lies straight and once a lie is told, it leads to other lies that must be remembered as well.

When you are tempted to lie your way to peace, resist. If (when) you find yourself in a situation that presents a dilemma between a lie and truth, ask yourself the following questions in response to the five principles above:

- Do I need to speak the truth in this situation or can I remain silent?

- If I need to speak, does it need to be now?

- Can I speak the truth in love?

- Can I speak the truth, recognizing that my perspective is one of many?

- What long-term objective will truth-telling gain me that lying will not?

People are looking to you for leadership. Don't sell your long-term influence for short-term peace. Peace founded on deception won't last and your leadership will be diminished.

Questions to consider:

1. Have you ever lied to keep the peace? Did it work? Would you encourage this practice among those you lead?

2. Who in your organization needs to hear these principles the most? How could you present this information in a way they would be inclined to hear?

3. Which principle related to truth-telling is the most challenging for you to accept? Why?

Chapter 15

Kill things. Have a funeral.
Celebrate their success. Move on.

Zombie Horses Will Kill You

I'm not into the zombie craze that has engulfed our media, but this image was introduced by a client and I thought it worth exploring. The popular concept of zombies is that the undead function as mindless enemies of the living. It is with this in mind that I introduce the image of zombie horses. We've all heard the expression "beating a dead horse." It has become a cliché. Thankfully, we are no longer drawn to the image being evoked, but simply translate the phrase into its intended equivalent - "You are continuing to discuss something that isn't worth the energy." This is how a cliché is born: When an imagistic phrase loses its power to evoke the corresponding image but leads one to simply translate the words into another phrase, it has become a cliché. That's why writing often suffers from mixed metaphors because no one is considering how the verbal images fail to align with one another.

The problem is that many organizations have halls filled with stampeding zombie horses - ideas that some in leadership are confident are dead and not worth discussing, while others continue to foster their undead survival with its mindless destruction. What is a leader to do with these issues that have been "resolved" but never quite go away?

Make sure that everyone is as clear as you are on the resolution of the issue.

Perhaps you simply have not articulated the resolution of the issue in a way that is clear and associated with your authority. People may be aware that this is your "opinion" on the topic or your "stance," but they fail to see that you have spoken in your role as organizational leader and that your statement is final. It's not uncommon to deliver bad or challenging news with qualifiers and language meant to soften the blow. Unfortunately, this often has the undesired effect of muddying the waters of clear communication.

Make sure that leaders within the organization subscribe to and practice a "disagree but commit" strategy.

Healthy organizations have leaders who disagree about issues, but who commit to one another that those disagreements will not leave the conference room, particularly once a decision has been made. This is not an "agree to disagree" mentality, as that implies ongoing division. Under "disagree but commit," leaders will *not* continue to build factions or to argue their case publicly but will fall in line with the organization's position on the topic. Leadership will speak with one voice. They may continue to debate the issue's implementation and evaluation of that implementation over time, but they will not lobby against the position of the organization.

Consider the value of insisting that a specific issue has been resolved versus letting it remain alive.

When you find a zombie horse, you must see that its status as undead changes. Either you make clear that the horse's demise has been prematurely communicated and it is still alive, or you make clear that the horse is, in fact, dead (the situation we've been discussing). There are times, however, when mere reference to a dead idea gives it an aura of life for those holding out hope of its survival. Sometimes just mentioning the horse is enough to sustain its zombie existence. Clarified death or continuing life is a judgment call you must make and one that may not be supported or appreciated by others around you, but that is the privilege of leadership - making challenging decisions with far-reaching implications.

Respond quickly and vigorously when someone in leadership is found to be keeping a stable of zombie horses at their disposal.

This destabilization of company perspective and lack of respect for fellow leaders must not be tolerated. Depending upon the severity of the offense and the vigor of the stable's inhabitants, this may require anything from a private reprimand to termination.

Zombie horses running wild within your organization can lead to an environment so toxic that all productivity and growth can grind to a halt. As with any infestation, the longer it is allowed to fester and grow, the more difficult it will be to stamp out. Commit to the elimination of zombie horses wandering your halls and bring the carnage to an end.

Questions to consider:

1. Are there easily identified zombie horses wandering your halls? What are they and what should be done in response?

2. Do you sometimes suffer from a lack of clear and precise communication? What are the implications for your organization? What must you do to be clear?

3. Who still needs to make the transition from "agree to disagree" to "disagree but commit," and how can you make sure that this happens?

Section 4

The Leader's Role: Driving Execution

Driving execution is part of leadership because having a vision and building alignment are not sufficient to bring a vision to pass. Behaviors must be pursued and achieved if the organization is to move toward the desired future. Many leaders want to skip alignment and jump straight to execution, but their efforts will be undermined by that strategy. Similarly, it may be tempting to host a vision reveal event to energize and motivate team members, but if the event isn't followed up with consistent effort in execution, the vision will be stillborn.

"A Brief Theory of Time" talks about taking action now, today, to continue organizational progress toward the vision.

"Words ARE Action" reminds leaders that execution isn't doing things versus saying things, but that saying *is* a form of doing that the leader must influence as part of execution.

"Lessons from the Aloha State" looks at principles of empowerment and decision-making that allow execution to be more likely and effective.

"Are you growing your business or going out of business?" provides a framework for business that encourages execution directed toward the vision.

"Life in a Disrupted World" challenges the leader to consider how business is evolving, recognizing that execution must evolve as well so that the vision is consistently pursued and realized.

Getting things done is where most leaders excel. Getting things done for the purpose of bringing vision to life is what matters.

Chapter 16

Remembering is fine,
dreaming is good,
but none of it matters
if you don't act now.

A Brief Theory of Time

Imagine a family whose eldest child has had his temporary driving permit for four days. And imagine that child is backing out of his long and winding driveway – one side has grass and a large pine tree, the other a retaining wall. Now imagine that child hitting the wall. Pondering this hypothetical (but all too real) situation has led me to articulate my brief theory of time. I trust you'll see that it applies to you, professionally and personally.

The Past: Regretters/Dwellers/Learners

Regretters: What might have been is often accompanied by feelings of regret. We wish our past could be different. In the situation I just described, it is tempting to wonder: How could the outcome have been avoided? The eldest child decided at the last minute to join members of the family headed to a movie and then asked to drive. What if he hadn't gone to the movie? The dad remembers that the last time he sat with his son as he backed out of the driveway, he pointed out that the son had strayed toward the grass and tree. What if he hadn't made that point - perhaps his son over-corrected because of those comments. The mom thinks about how she almost yelled at her son to watch the wall but chose not to because he had already been corrected numerous times in his first four days of driving. What if she had yelled? Regret is an all-too-natural response to what happened, focusing on what might have been.

Dwellers: If you've ever attended a high school reunion, you've met the dwellers - the people whose best years are in the past. They keep trying to recreate them and make them real so that they never have to leave. Think "Glory Days" by Bruce Springsteen. At bottom, dwelling is missing out on what is and still might be.

Learners: We cannot change our past, but we can be changed by our past. That is the insight of the learners, those who understand that life's journey continues and that they need to grow from their successes as well as their mistakes. Regretting changes nothing about our past, but it can keep us from acting now with courage. Dwelling is an illusion that can't be maintained - it's like trying to have a picnic in the middle of an interstate; even if you manage to draw others in, you cannot stop the flow around you.

The Future: Worriers/Dreamers/Planners

Worriers: Back to our student driver - now that he has had his first accident within his first four days of driving, it is easy to wonder about his future. If he cannot successfully escape the driveway, how can he navigate through traffic? What might be is often aligned with a sense of worry. We hope that our future turns out the way we are trying to make it. We are seeking control where none is available.

Dreamers: Others dream - they can write or talk a good future, but essentially, they are asleep. They are doing nothing to bring about the reality they hope to experience. Dreams don't come true by chance, it is planning and action that make them real.

Planners: We cannot act in our future, but we can act for our future. Planners have learned that it is possible to make decisions today that guide our steps in the desired direction. We do not control our future, our circumstances, or the free choices of others, but we can have influence that makes our future better than if we were coasting or driving in reverse. Like regret, worry changes nothing, but it can keep us from acting with courage. Like dwelling, dreaming is an illusion that cannot be maintained.

NOW: Acting in the Present

Actors: This moment we call "now" - this is the only moment when we are able to act. That doesn't mean that the past and future aren't significant to our activity in the present, they are.

We need to live now by learning from the past and acting in the light of our desired future. Just remember that we sometimes rewrite our past to support our preferred perspective - whether positive or negative. As for the future, the light shines brightest on the next few hours and days, dimming quickly as we move farther into the future. We may talk about 10 years from now, but whether it is our organization's growth, the federal budget, peace in the Middle East, the college experience of our children, our next career, or blessed retirement, looking 10 years out is like trying to see your feet while standing in Lake Erie - you know your toes are there, but you find yourself staring into murky darkness, your feet obscured within the inky cloud. (At least that was Lake Erie in my youth. Perhaps it's gotten clearer.)

This moment is what you have - make the most of it. Act now. Cast off regret - the car is already damaged. Abandon dwelling - there's another trip to take today. Resist worry - the outcome of his next trip is yet to be determined, in part, by circumstances and the free will of others - both beyond our control. Wake up and quit simply dreaming - eventually his driving must take place in reality, on the pavement. See what he has learned from his experience, plan a better approach to avoiding both tree and wall, and then hand him the keys.

Leaders are not only people of vision who take time to build alignment among key stakeholders, they drive the execution needed to bring that vision into reality. Learn from your past. Plan for your future. Act today!

Questions to consider:

1. When considering the past, what regrets are anchoring you in place? What do you dwell on that keeps you firmly stuck, unable to move forward?

2. Are there specific worries that you need to release to improve your outlook? Are you asleep and dreaming, or are you planning practical steps that will guide your future?

3. What keeps you from acting decisively in the present? What will you do to free yourself to act now? Do you need the help of a friend or colleague in this process?

Chapter 17

Don't underestimate the significance of words to you and your organization - words matter.

Words ARE Action!

Daily I drive past the middle school our children attended. Someone at the school chooses motivational phrases to put on the school's sign and periodically I slow sufficiently to read them as I pass. Consider these phrases I have seen recently: "Words may get you attention, but your actions build your reputation;" "People who care use words to express, people who care more use their actions;" and my personal favorite, "People will judge you by your actions, not your words. You may have a heart of gold, but so does a hard-boiled egg." A quick search of the Internet demonstrates that this sentiment has strong precedent and good company. Consider the following statements exalting doing over saying:

- *"Well done is better than well said."* Benjamin Franklin

- *"After all is said and done, a lot more will have been said than done."* Author Unknown

- *"Trust only movement. Life happens at the level of events, not of words. Trust movement."* Alfred Adler

- *"Talk doesn't cook rice."* Chinese Proverb

A clarification followed by a challenge. . .

While it is unarguable that "talk doesn't cook rice," there is a sense in which *no* rice has ever been cooked apart from speech (written and spoken). People are taught from one generation to the next how to cook rice, they are given reasons - logical, emotional, cultural, dietary - for why they should cook rice, and so on. Words - whether spoken or written or pantomimed - are actions. What we do apart from words may not always align with what we say and that may be a form of hypocrisy. Talking about things is not the same as doing them, but while that's perceived to be a negative when talking about great deeds, it's a source of comfort to parents that our kids don't really "burn down the school" on a bad day. So, talk without corresponding action can be both a blessing and a curse.

Abraham Lincoln is remembered not only for leading this nation but for the words he used in doing so. His words produced results and responses and actively influence behavior to this day. The Emancipation Proclamation was an action, but it was the carefully selected words that achieved what Lincoln intended - the freeing of slaves in every area of the Union that his administration did not control, without extending freedom to those slaves held in parts of the country supportive of the Union (read it carefully to see this politically judicious impact).

Let's end this nonproductive and misleading divide between words and actions and recognize that words are one form of activity. As I've noted before, when we tell children "sticks and stones may break my bones, but words will never hurt me" we are, all of us, liars. Sometimes I would have preferred a pelting with rocks over the hurtful words that have left indelible scars.

Each day treat your words with the care they deserve. Think before speaking and definitely think before hitting "Send." Consider how your words can be used to bless others. Many leaders tell me they are not as free with praise as they know they should be. Handwrite notes of thanks to your team members, stop by a team member's desk and tell them specifically how they have contributed to the success of the team today, single out in front of others those who are comfortable with public praise, call team members by name, and look for opportunities to thank those who often go unnoticed - the cleaning crew member, the parking attendant, the building security, and so on.

Use your words as another form of action by which you can shape and influence the world around you. Then with me you can say:

- *"Well said and well done is better than merely well done."*

- *"After all is said and done, a lot has been done in the saying as well as the doing."*

- *"Events and words both produce movement. Trust movement."*

- *"Rice doesn't get cooked apart from words."*

Remember, execution is driven by words that inspire and motivate others.

Questions to consider:

1. Think of a time when your words landed you in hot water; how did you handle the fallout? What did you learn from this experience that helped to shape your words from that point forward?

2. Do you believe that you achieve consistent harmony between your words and your actions? In what areas of your life is this alignment most difficult to maintain?

3. How do you bless others through your words? What should you do to be more effective in these efforts?

Chapter 18

Customer service excellence isn't an accident, but the result of intentional choices.

Lessons from the Aloha State

My wife and I returned from a team-building trip to Hawaii, renewed and ready to address the opportunities and challenges of daily life. On our trip, I observed six principles in evidence around us.

1) Customer service heroes need authority to make real decisions

We bought snorkeling equipment for this trip so that we wouldn't be dependent upon a tour operator or rental store each time we wanted to enter the water. My only problem was with my mask. I experienced consistent, slow leakage. I Googled experts and read advice on how this could be avoided. Finally, I went to a dive shop to ask for help. The manager observed, "You have a fairly large noggin." He tried several masks on me and then pointed in the direction of his generic rental mask. "One reason we use this mask with a wide range of renters is that it fits most faces." He sold me the mask for a few dollars more than his cost (and far less than I had anticipated spending), shared with us his passion for diving, and sent us on our way. He was even willing for me to return the mask should it not fit properly, charging me only his daily rental fee. Here was a man whose passion, honesty, and knowledge of his product, combined with his delegated authority to decide, resulted in a superior customer service experience. If you want to lead a team of customer service heroes, give your people freedom to make decisions that benefit your organization and your customer. Of course, this example is predicated on a significant level of trust between leader and team member.

2) Your vision may be clearer from another perspective or on another day

My wife and I got up one morning at 2:30 AM to drive to the summit of Haleakala. There you may witness some of the most amazing sunrises known to man. What we experienced was a windy, rainy, chilly morning – nothing like the brochures that entice you to make the trip. Later that week we took a helicopter tour of Maui and saw Haleakala from above. This time, the volcanic crater and surrounding areas were clearly visible. Sometimes in life we can't see the path before us. We may need to elevate our view, involve the expertise of others (a helicopter pilot in our case), or recognize that what is cloudy and obscured one day, may be clear and visible on another.

3) Differing values motivate differing behaviors

We spent several days on the island of Molokai. One of the least visited islands, Molokai reminded us of visits to third world regions. The people were friendly to us as visitors, but many have made their opposition to development of the island quite clear. A guidebook noted that it is difficult to write about the businesses on Molokai because they come and go so frequently. An oceanfront golf resort near our condo was boarded up and the golf course completely overgrown. It is just one of the many development efforts that has come and gone. "Keep Molokai, Molokai" was a slogan seen on signs and cars and is the title of a song by a popular local musician. On an island with pristine beaches that are virtually uninhabited, shops that look like they haven't been updated in decades, food that is crazy expensive, and regionally high unemployment, you'd think there would be a greater interest in development.

Progress vs. preservation is a powerful struggle and one that cannot be resolved apart from appeal to underlying values. Sometimes in life it seems obvious that additional employment opportunities would be good for a group of people - how could they think otherwise? They may not value the material benefits that drive so many of us and may resent watching many of the resources generated by local enterprises leaving their communities to the benefit of outsiders. Be careful: Obvious solutions to problems may not be so obvious to people with differing values who don't agree on what problems are to be solved, what solutions will work, and who should provide those solutions.

4) You can drive people's behaviors through benefits and opportunities

When we checked into our hotel for our final night before returning to the mainland, there were three lines. Registration for the masses, registration for the hotel's elite members, and registration for those who had checked in online. The first line stretched through the open-air lobby and was filled with people who looked tired and discouraged. The elite line was long but moving and people appeared hopeful that they might still get to the pool before dinner. The online check-in line was, well, there was no line. I asked what I needed to do for online check-in, fired up my hotel app, and immediately became next in line. We were seated in our beachfront restaurant having a late lunch while some of the people were still registering. You want people to join your rewards program? You want people to download your app? You want people to check in online? Then drive those behaviors through corresponding benefits and opportunities.

5) Names are easy, living up to them is the challenge

We chose a transportation provider with the word "Speedy" in its company name to pick us up at the airport, take us to our hotel, and then return us to the airport the next day. At both ends of the process, the shuttle was anything but "Speedy." The delays did not significantly impact our stay or our ability to make our outgoing flight, but given the prominence of "Speedy" in the name, they felt like delays and led us to remark more than once that the shuttle wasn't "Speedy" at all. Pick names of organizations, products, and roles with care, because they help to create expectations in your customers' minds. The catchy name begs the question: Do you live up to it?

6) Choosing to bless the other

It has been noted that in great marriages, each partner believes that he or she has gotten the better part of the bargain. My wife and I spent our time away focusing on ways that we could bless the other. In the past, I have said that the only problem with a beach vacation is the sand, sun, and saltwater. This time I was ready for each foray into the deep. In part, it's because my wife is my best friend and I want to bless her. In part, it was because she was blessing me.

There are people who believe that focusing on the blessing of others is a sign of weakness that only leads to being taken advantage of. I'm here to tell you that the strongest relationships are ones where people allow themselves to be taken advantage of in the pursuit of their larger objectives and as an expression of their values. That's one of the reasons we love certain retailers

- they allow themselves to be taken advantage of repeatedly through their ridiculously generous return policies; policies that further their customer service reputations, the number of visits to their stores, and sales of their products. They achieve their objectives by choosing to bless others.

Questions to consider:

1. Which of these six principles resonates most with your current situation?

2. Is there a specific principle that you need to focus on to improve your organization? How might you go about implementing it?

3. Whom do you need to choose to bless to achieve your objectives (or just for the sake of the blessing)? How might you be taken advantage of in the process and is that risk worth the potential outcome?

Chapter 19

Be hungry and know your ideal client.

Are You Growing Your Business or Going Out of Business?

Life doesn't allow us to stand still - we are moving whether we like it or not. Even if we manage to slow down or somehow stop ourselves, everything else will keep going around us. The question to ask is whether we are moving effectively to our target. Let's look at four areas that can help you assess your progress.

#1: Serve and Grow

When I first started my business, I went into every conversation with two words in my mind - "serve" and "grow." I wanted to make sure that I was focused on serving the needs of those I met, and I wanted to grow from these interactions. Serving meant really listening to them, their stories, their backgrounds, their personality types and preferences. It also meant asking lots of questions - sometimes questions that appeared intrusive or even off-subject, but questions designed to uncover the information I needed to serve them effectively. The second word, "grow", was intended for me in these conversations. I wanted to make sure that I remained a lifelong learner, that I never got comfortable or thought I knew it all, but that I was always learning from others. When I was first hired as a youth pastor, I called everyone I knew in youth ministry to ask questions about my new role. Within nine months, people were calling me. I've seen how quickly a person can move from being viewed as a novice to being seen as an expert and the trap that becomes as it stunts one's growth and maturity. Keep learning and keep admitting that you need to learn.

#2: Operations/Service/Marketing

It quickly became apparent why so many people start businesses and so few persist successfully. There are three key elements to any business: operations, service, and marketing. The terms may be different in your world, but the principles are the same. There are tasks required to keep the business running - like paying bills, having business cards designed and printed, and keeping your e-mail server up and running. You've got to take care of the clients (or whatever you may call them) that you have currently, and you've got to figure out how to keep new clients coming. Many people are good at one or two of these, but when they neglect the third, the business can only survive for so long before it implodes (or, less dramatically, withers). As organizations grow, they can hire people as specialists in each of these areas and, if not careful, people within the organization can forget why employees in these other areas are necessary. Teachers really can lose sight of the possibility that a school district may wither over time from lack of students.

#3: Owner vs. Employee

People need to recognize whether they prefer being an owner or an employee and, then, whether they are cut out to be or can become what they prefer. I am an owner at heart and that has been reflected in my career path, even through the many years that technically I was an employee. The real question in starting my business was whether I could operate effectively as an owner without a regular paycheck. You may feel strongly that you are one or the other, but if you don't have the knowledge, ability, or experience to fill this role, then you've likely failed before leaving the gate.

#4: Ideal Client

There are three stages in the development of any business. The first stage is desperation - you will do anything you can if someone is willing to write a check. The second is hunger - being more selective about your clients, but always wanting to grow. The final stage is complacency - assuming the stream of clients is ever-flowing. This is the stage that often precedes going out of business. A warning sign that complacency is a threat to your organization is when you assume the retention of your ideal clients without providing the excellent service that drew them to you. An important principle for a growing business is that retaining good clients is easier than gaining new ones.

I knew I needed to make the move from being desperate to being hungry, without ever losing the desire for growth that went with desperation. I love my clients and, as I always say, am committed to their professional and personal success. However, when you're desperate, it may not be clear who your clients will be, let alone your ideal clients.

In my world, an ideal client has the following six characteristics:

1. They are self-aware leaders who surround themselves with those having complementary strengths;

2. They are committed to professional and personal success;

3. They lead organizations structured as teams;

4. They and the teams they head are recognized by their peers as successful;

5. They are continually growing and improving, both individually and corporately; and

6. They invest resources (time, money, personnel) into the ongoing success of the organization.

This is not to say that we will not work with clients lacking one of these characteristics, but that part of moving from desperate to hungry means that we recognize where we tend to be most successful (of greatest value to our clients) and so we look for individuals and organizations that meet these criteria.

Questions to consider:

1. In what areas are you clearly moving forward? Is your speed appropriate?

2. How do you define and measure growth within your organization? How do you define and measure growth in your personal life?

3. Is there any significant area of your professional or personal life in which you are becoming complacent? What do you need to do to get it growing again?

Chapter 20

*Anticipate disruption or
get out of the way.*

Life in a Disrupted World

We live in a disrupted world. Is the evidence of this statement difficult to find? Everywhere you look, life is in a consistent state of disruption. Our sleep is disrupted by worry, our daily commute is disrupted by congested traffic, our work is disrupted by greater demands and, often, shrinking pay, industry is disrupted by innovative ideas and changing technology, and the list goes on. What I've found is that my clients face disruptive forces in their industries. Here are four examples, followed by four possible responses.

Financial Services

The broker of yesteryear has become the financial advisor or financial planner of today. Transactional business has given way to fee-based services that provide recurring revenue. The disruption is arising from technology that aids the do-it-yourselfer, as well as forces that keep pressuring the fees that are charged to clients. Faced with shrinking profits margins and increasing client access to virtual resources, this is an industry experiencing growing pains like never before.

Education

K-12 public education is rated as poor or failing in many communities. Colleges and graduate schools are seeing the liberal arts model continuously assaulted. The K-12 disruption is arising from homeschooling and charter schools, that along with private schools, compete with public schools for students and funding. Disruption to higher education comes in the form of professional training and distance education. Even on the campuses of "liberal arts colleges" the most popular majors are now business, communications, psychology, education, nursing, and other professional degrees. Our son attended a university of 19,000, of which just 3,000 are traditional undergraduates on a residential campus.

Churches

Traditional churches are adapting worship styles, venues, and length of services to keep the faith-filled in the pews. The disruption is arising from parachurch organizations that provide many of the elements of churches without the all-encompassing commitment to community that some find unnecessary and from those who have "outgrown" the church altogether. Donald Miller, author of bestseller *Blue Like Jazz*, says he does not attend church regularly. In fact, he writes: "Most of the influential Christian leaders I know (who are not pastors) do not attend church."

Healthcare

Where do I even start? Hospitals are going under in some locales and being gobbled up elsewhere as they seek to survive in a world of shrinking reimbursements and increasing expectations. The disruption is arising from concierge providers built around fee-based services, from smaller niche hospitals, and from larger competitors who must consume or die; all within a world lacking clear direction or sense of what will be. Insurance and the government's role in healthcare further complicate this picture.

Response

So, what are we to do? Here are four responses to living life in a disrupted world.

1. **Hope** your career comes to a close before the disruption takes root and you go the way of travel agents. If you can get out in time, perhaps the disruption can pass you by with minimal impact.

2. **Change** careers to escape the coming tsunami. Young people today are expected to have as many as seven

careers in their lifetime, but many of us find that prospect wearying rather than invigorating.

3. **Adjust** with the disruption incrementally as required or get out in front of the changes and become a disrupter. If you can't beat them, join them.

4. **Continue** your current path, believing there will always be a place for some blacksmiths shoeing horses, some people who make travel arrangements for others, some transactional brokers, as well as some traditional churches, hospitals, and schools.

Humanity will always need a way to build and preserve wealth, to educate and train, to impart faith, and to care for the needs of the body. What each field looks like in 20 years is unknown. What is certain is that each of those fields will be further disrupted by technology and evolving cultural forces. Only time will tell, but at some point, you must decide how you will respond and then learn to live with the consequences of those decisions.

Of course, as a leader, this can never be just about you. Leadership is a one-to-many relationship, encompassing Vision, Alignment, and Execution. So, retiring or escaping before the disruption upends your world is too limited a strategy. You have accepted the call to include others in this equation. You are left with responses #3 and #4 from the list above. Choose wisely!

Again, Pontious comes through. *"I was left wanting more advice from you here. A bit more about how to adjust or continue. This chapter feels like you pinned a $20 to my chest, dropped me off at the bus station, and said good luck!"*

Typically, I encourage clients to **Continue** as they **Adjust**. Unless you are creative enough to genuinely disrupt an industry, it is better to watch for the coming wave, looking to stay just ahead of it rather than getting too far out in front or crushed beneath it as it crashes. For example, the financial advising industry is going to continue experiencing fee compression. I urge clients to have trigger mechanisms in place for when they need to reduce fees without doing so before it's necessary.

Questions to consider:

1. Where is your life experiencing disruption right now? How have you responded?

2. Has disruption in your industry caused your organization to undergo significant change? What were those changes and how did they impact your organization? How did the changes and their implementation impact morale?

3. When has disruption led to positive change for you and your organization? What made that positive change possible? Was it something that organizational leaders influenced or controlled?

Section 5

The Leader's Success

We all die - without exception. So, in what ways will your life have mattered? How will your character and the pursuit of vision have influenced others for good? It's time to contemplate success and to self-evaluate as we consider our leadership scorecard.

"What Is Success?" asks you to define "success" for yourself and to consider how that definition should impact your choices and be expressed through your behavior.

"Gaining the Most from Your Competition" stresses the need for comparing ourselves to the appropriate reference group when considering our success.

"Then Came a Pharaoh" reminds the leader that change is inevitable and that even if what you build to last fails to endure, you may be a success.

"Pursuing Goals Worthy of a Human Life" challenges leaders to compete for prizes that matter.

"Transitional Spaces" prepares the leader for the realities of transition so that it can be celebrated rather than mourned.

Jesus asked, "What does it profit a man to gain the world, if he loses his soul? What can a man give in exchange for his soul?" Make sure that when all is said and done, what you have said and done was worth saying and doing.

Chapter 21

*Define "success" and pursue
your definition without distraction.*

What is Success?

"Are you successful?" Perhaps you'll offer my favorite answer: "It depends." In what area of life? Compared to what/to whom? The beauty of success is that it is within your power to determine the standard by which you will be measured. Often, however, we allow others to tell us what success is - we allow our parents, spouse, co-workers, peers, and friends to define our goals.

A pastor who played a prominent role in his community once told me, "I wish I had spent more time with my children." My response: "You can't have it both ways. You wouldn't be where you are today in terms of influence if you had chosen to spend more time with your children. Would you have been willing to give this up?" It's easy to sit back and reflect, playing the "what if" game. The reality is, at some point you decided to go down a certain path to pursue goals you believed to be worth achieving. This choice, by default, either eliminated or at least impacted your ability to obtain other goals down alternate paths. In the previous scenario, the person's "success" as a pastor may be judged differently than his "success" as a parent, depending on whom you ask and the criteria that are emphasized.

To determine whether you are successful, you need to answer three questions:

1. What do you want out of life? Go through the various areas of your life and determine what you are seeking to accomplish.

2. Is what you are seeking worthy of your life? Reflect on your goals to determine their worth.

3. How are you doing moving toward the goals you've identified? List the markers you have completed that evidence your progress toward these goals.

In looking at the first question, it comes as no surprise that people want different things out of life. A college student once told me that she wanted to be married four times (personally I'm content with once). She wanted to experience life with different people having different personalities and perspectives. I told her that, in all fairness, she should make sure Husband #1 was aware of this goal.

The answer to the second question depends unavoidably on your subjective values. People have given their lives to many different causes and purposes. What you think worthy of your life might not impress me at all. My life purpose is "freeing people to be themselves." My wife thinks I'm automatically a success since people, by definition, are themselves. Obviously, I have a somewhat more substantive sense in mind - helping people find who they are called to be, how they are wired, and why they are on this planet. Many people are never free in this sense; they never become themselves, but spend their lives trying to become someone they are not.

Answering the third question involves evaluation and measurement. It is essential that our goals are behavioral and not mere abstractions that can never be defined or progress toward them measured. Personally, I don't find it a problem that some goals are never reached if you continue making progress toward them. We may fail to reach a goal, but are successful nonetheless. I wanted to complete my PhD by the time I was 30. Instead I spent three years in ministry and completed it at the age of 32. Those three years changed my life for the better and made the delayed achievement well worth it.

Are you successful? You must answer that question for yourself and may have different answers for different areas of your life. Others may answer this question about you based on their definitions, but you are not required to accept those evaluations. Of course, if your boss has a definition of "success" for your employment, you might benefit from knowing and fulfilling it. This is true of all relational commitments (e.g., marriage).

My concern? Don't spend your life chasing a definition of "success" that is ultimately unfulfilling or unrelated to who you are. "But how do I know it's unfulfilling before I arrive?" Researching the destination and communicating with others who have chosen and reached it before you, making sure that the place they describe is where you hope to arrive. Just as you might research a resort prior to a vacation without being guaranteed that it will be all that you hope for, so the satisfaction of achieving a particular success cannot be guaranteed. Don't arrive at the destination only to find that neither it nor the trip were worth your effort and investment.

Questions to consider:

1. Take the time to go through the three questions posed above. What do you want out of life? Are your objectives compatible with the goals of those closest to you?

2. Is what you are seeking worthy of your life? [Consider the challenges in Chapter 24, "Pursuing Goals Worthy of a Human Life."]

3. How are you doing in moving toward the goals you've identified? What sacrifices do you need to make to succeed and are you willing to make them?

Chapter 22

Winning isn't everything,
but it should be something.

Gaining the Most from Your Competition

For eight years, our family was in Indianapolis for the Bands of America Grand Nationals where our successive children's bands competed against more than a hundred high school marching units from across the nation. One year our high school band advanced to the semifinal round before being eliminated. What I appreciated was our band director's comments at the year-end brunch following the competition. He made the point that while we didn't win, it was an honor to compete alongside the top bands and to continue learning from what others brought to their shows. This is a not-so-well-kept secret in any athletic arena: If you want to be the best, you must play the best. Consider these quotes:

"I've failed over and over again in my life and that is why I succeed." – Michael Jordan

"Never quit. It is the easiest cop-out in the world. Set a goal and don't quit until you attain it. When you do attain it, set another goal, and don't quit until you reach it. Never quit." – Bear Bryant

Success and failure are not end goals for those that choose to be champions. Michael Jordan spent his entire career using his failures to motivate, learn, and grow. Like him or not, no one can argue his place among the greatest ever to have played the game of basketball. Legendary coach Bear Bryant similarly recognizes that while attaining a goal (success) is a worthy pursuit, the champion doesn't stop there. They use their success as a springboard toward even greater achievements. Engaging in competition against an opponent that you can clearly dominate, while perhaps providing a fleeting sense of satisfaction, will not lead on to greatness. Development doesn't happen when effort is not needed. Sure, your record may look great at the end of the season, but what have you really accomplished? If you want to become the best, you need to acknowledge the following three facets of achievement.

Facet #1: You are competing

Sometimes my not-for-profit clients prefer not to think of themselves as competing with others, but they are. Schools are working to attract the best students and athletes. Churches, at the very least, are competing for people's attention and attendance. Even hospitals are competing for patients, as evidenced by the radio commercials for heart and cancer centers. My for-profit clients, like the many financial advisors with whom I work, are keenly aware that they are competing each and every day. We all compete, every day. Whether it's for time, attention, recognition, promotion, validation or any one of a hundred other counters, we are competing. The sooner we recognize and accept this, the sooner we can get moving in a more focused and determined direction.

Facet #2: You don't have to come in first to be a winner

No, I am not some advocate of score-free soccer games or participation trophies for everyone. I just happen to believe that winning doesn't always necessitate being in first place. There is a longer perspective to life in which continuous learning and improvement are the goal. Often the competitions we enter are short-term endeavors that we may or may not "win." However, if you adopt a longer-term perspective that says, "I may not have won, but I'm walking away improved in some specific way," you are still advancing toward greater victory. When you compete against the best, there will be opportunity to learn and grow, even at the cost of a temporary loss. You win by competing against the best and pushing yourself to be better (although, keep reading for further clarification of "best").

Facet #3: You need to compare yourself with the proper reference group

One mistake many people make is to compare themselves

against the wrong competitors. If you are a rural high school with 300 students, your reference group is probably not the urban school of thousands. In golf, Phil Mickelson does himself no good by comparing himself to the average high school golfer. Likewise, the weekend duffer shouldn't use members of the Ryder Cup team as his reference group. It's too easy to be a winner or a loser if you aren't looking to the right people as your competition. Choose a reference group that challenges you to grow and to perform at your highest level without leaving you demoralized. Compete against the best among your properly calibrated reference group.

Questions to consider:

1. Who is your competition? Do you need to consider "bumping up" to a higher level? How would you do that and what benefits might be realized?

2. Are you comparing yourself and your company to the proper reference group? How do you make that determination and are you recalibrating regularly over time?

3. Reflect on a time when you didn't come in first, but still won. How did this come about? What lessons did you learn?

Chapter 23

Find your place within the
inevitability of change.

"Then Came a Pharaoh"

In the early 90s, I was attending an academic conference when I heard the speaker quote the Old Testament, specifically Exodus chapter 1, verse 8, as a way of addressing institutional change and people's surprise when old securities are stripped away.

"Then came a pharaoh who knew not Joseph." Exodus 1:8

As a quick refresher, Joseph had risen to a place of great power within Egypt, despite his rather challenging early life. He had been sold into slavery by his brothers and then spent years in an Egyptian prison. Eventually, Joseph occupied the number two spot in Egypt, second only to Pharaoh himself. This status gave him enormous influence and power that allowed him to save both his family and the nation from starvation. But, as they inevitably do, things changed. Along came a new Pharaoh who didn't know Joseph, and nothing was ever the same. Privilege gave way to persecution. Distinction was replaced by disregard. The old became the new and the new was undesirable. Worse, it was undeserved. Joseph's descendants were seen as a threat to the security of Egypt, and so, an entire community went from decision-makers to slaves.

Sometimes we think we're going to change the world, or at least our portion of it, but the world and its institutions have a way of resisting and humbling our efforts. In fact, our efforts may even be resented. So, should we just give up, be fatalists, and accept our lot? No, but can we reframe our expectations so that we impact those within our sphere of influence? Here are four principles for finding one's place within the life of an organization.

Principle #1: Organizations outlive leaders

We need to remember that the organization outlives the individuals who make it up and serve its purposes. If the organization doesn't outlive your leadership, then you've got a whole other set of problems. Your goal always needs to be the long-term growth and success of the organization and cannot be limited to the time that you will serve, with no thought or care for the future.

Principle #2: Influence has a shelf-life

We should attempt to effect change that makes a difference in our lives and the lives of others, without fooling ourselves into believing that we are creating a new permanence impervious to future change. Look around your community at buildings named for leaders of previous generations that are now forgotten. Or consider Vita Radium Suppositories that were marketed in the early 1900's and guaranteed to contain real radium as a life-giving health aid. Today, it's hard to imagine this idea ever making sense. Wouldn't it be nice if our every decision was unanimously cheered, knowing that our influence is so great, not even future generations will question it? Get over it. Life doesn't work that way and there will always be someone bigger, stronger, or smarter waiting to take our place. Seize the opportunity you have now to make a difference and let those in the future construct the best world available to them.

Principle #3: Focus on your sphere

We should be realistic in our attempts to influence the organization and, through it, the world around us. Just as the last principle was a warning about time, this is a warning about space or sphere of influence. Yes, there have been people and inventions that have changed the world: The printing press, the electric light bulb, and duct tape, just to name a few. If you are CEO of a company or President of the United States, your primary goal needs to be to use your leadership to produce positive change for those you serve, rather than trying to change the entirety - all that has gone before and all that is to follow. I strongly believe that if we focus our efforts in this way, it's possible that what we accomplish may very well resonate far outside our limited scope. However, if we start with our eyes too far down the road, we may never reach our destination at all.

Principle #4: Celebrate seasons of successful trajectory

Keep the trajectory of the organization moving in a positive direction and release the need to arrive, to finish, to complete its work. Momentum may seem at times like wading through knee-deep mud and it can be frustrating when progress is slower than you believe possible. In addition to never reaching an endpoint, it's often discouraging to realize that the success you do achieve may be only for a season. Just keep moving, because one day there will be a new Pharaoh, with new ideas, and your work may be undone. While enduring success is the ideal objective, it's rarely possible. Don't accept a judgment that you were unsuccessful when change comes, and it will. Your success may have been for a season, but for that season you kept your organization moving in the right direction and for that season your success was real.

Questions to consider:

1. Think of a time when you were subjected to change in the leadership above you. Was the transition smooth? How did it impact you and the organization?

2. In the example you just considered, how could the transition have been handled more effectively? What difference would that have made for you and others within the organization?

3. Have you ever been the new Pharaoh? What have you learned about implementing transition when you are the leader?

Chapter 24

When your life is over,
will it have been worth living?

Pursuing Goals Worthy of a Human Life

Primary and secondary goals

To begin, I would make a distinction between primary and secondary goals. Primary goals are those worthy of your life. These have to do with your purpose, your calling, the reason you have been placed on this planet. They often focus on caring for others beyond yourself. Secondary goals are not sufficient for a human life. They have to do with your lifestyle, your interests, the pursuits you believe will make your life enjoyable.

Once I turn to concrete examples, you and I are unlikely to agree on which goals are primary and which are secondary, but allow me to try and illustrate this distinction. I would contend that becoming a millionaire by the age of 30 is not worthy of your life, but within the context of your calling, it may be a perfectly appropriate secondary goal. Commitment to weekly participation in a community of faith can be worthy of your life when it contributes to your sense of purpose and calling, helping you to see why you specifically have been placed on this planet, and allowing you to serve others in some meaningful way.

161

Why does this distinction matter? Because the goals that you determine are primary for your life reveal your priorities, influence the investment of your time, and determine how you interact with others - both those you love and those who appear only briefly along your journey.

Ambition or Hypocrisy?

Striving for more than you can achieve in this lifetime is not hypocrisy. The people I find attractive are those who are pursuing a life larger than what they have yet learned to live. They may be teenagers or senior citizens. This is not about the size of your influence or number of social media followers, it is about growth, learning, willingness to change, and a commitment to contributing to the lives of others. The danger for some is that vision exceeds their reach and so they will call people to live lives they themselves have not yet lived and may never live. To some, this smacks of hypocrisy.

Hypocrisy, for me, is more about the arrogance of self-deception and the façade one erects for the benefit of others. It contrasts with the humility of realizing there is more to life than we are capable of living fully, and that this is still worth pursuing and calling others to pursue. If you were to pay an entrance fee to tour a celebrity mansion, you would not expect full access to the entire grounds and every room in the house. You will see only a portion, a snapshot that someone has determined is worth showing. Much of the rest will remain off-limits and private for the owner and family. Yet somehow in our intrusive media culture, we expect to be given full-access tours of people's lives. We accuse them of hypocrisy if they retain some privacy, and then accuse them of hypocrisy when we are granted access to the basement and see defects that detract from our surface impression.

All of us have elements of our lives that we are working to improve which, in their current state, detract from our overall purpose and image. Some level of impression management is appropriate and to be expected.

This is the distinction I make between parents who want their children to live better lives (in every sense) and those who call their children to live lives better than they are *willing* to live. The former provide loving encouragement, while the latter are hypocrites. This same principle would apply to coaches and players, bosses and employees, supervisors and subordinates, the list goes on.

I consistently remind my clients, "I'm committed to your professional and personal success!" I have no qualms about helping clients pursue secondary goals, but I am interested to see that such goals are consistent with their primary goals and the larger perspective that gives their lives meaning and purpose.

Perhaps you don't need to hire a coach, but you do need someone in your life to help you in this endeavor. It's also possible that you may play this role for another. Either way, most of us need a partner when pursuing goals worthy of a human life.

Questions to consider:

1. Are you pursuing goals worthy of a human life? What are your primary goals?

2. What are some changes you need to make in your life to align your primary and secondary goals? Is there evidence of hypocrisy you need to address?

3. Do your daily actions contribute positively to others' pursuit of life-worthy goals? What do you need to do to support others and yourself in this pursuit of integrity (i.e., the absence of hypocrisy)?

Chapter 25

*Just because no one calls,
doesn't mean you weren't
a successful leader.*

Transitional Spaces

Each of us experiences transition during our career. We earn a new position within the same organization, we move from one organization to another, or we transition from full-time employment to some form of retirement. I want to share eight transition principles based on my work with those who have made this movement, particularly from full-time leadership to another stage of life.

#1: Transitional time is experienced differently depending upon one's perspective

The person leaving an organization will feel that a transition out of leadership is happening too quickly. There is more to teach one's successor and more to accomplish toward the goals one had set. The person entering this leadership position will feel that the transition happens far too slowly. There is energy and creative ideas needing to be unleashed, but none of this can happen until the current leader steps away. Both leaders need to purpose that these differing perspectives on time will not damage the transition and continuity within the organization.

#2: Your influence goes over a cliff

The individual leaving an organization will cling to the belief that people will call seeking their counsel and years of wisdom. This may happen over quiet lunches, away from the limelight, but those who take the reins *will* call. Reality? No one will call. No one will seek your counsel or ask for your accumulated wisdom. Your influence goes over a cliff. It does not recede at a gentle pace.

#3: You are not the organization

Leaders often take criticism of an organization personally, because over time, they see themselves as having become their organizations. Wise leaders recognize that this linkage of personal and organizational identity is unhealthy. The organization typically outlasts the leader (certainly this is what a healthy leader desires) and many of its issues and strengths belong to the organization and not to any one person.

#4: Leave a legacy and not merely a functioning organization

Leaving an organization prepared for its next leader and for the changes that will inevitably come, is a great accomplishment. It is handing off success from one generation to the next. It is *succession*. Leaving an organization with a culture that endures from generation to generation, with a set of values and a way of doing things that embodies those values, requires intentionality and discipline. It is leaving a legacy or preserving the legacy that you inherited as leader.

#5: Leave well

Knowing **when** to leave is critical. Knowing **how** to leave and choosing to do it that way requires humility. A great leader sets up the next leader for success. He handles many of the challenges faced by the organization before leaving, while having the discipline to not make sweeping changes as he walks out the door. He hands his successor an opportunity primed for success. Often this means that observers will credit the new leader with great vision and turning the organization around, when this transformation would have been less likely to happen and unlikely to succeed without the humility of the leader who walks away. Be prepared for this and just deal with it.

#6: Find your next act

There's a great deal of emphasis these days on retiring **to** something rather than simply retiring **from** something. For some people, this next act looks like something entirely new, while for others it is a continuation or an evolution of what they have been doing. Dieter Tasso started performing for the Tommy Bartlett Show in Wisconsin at the age of 44. That was pretty old to be standing on a slack wire stacking teacups and saucers on his head after tossing them from his foot. Bartlett noted that Tasso was actually quite humorous and told him: "You have the potential to be an unbelievably great comic. My suggestion is to continue to work more on your humorous patter, and your act will survive a lot longer than it would if you only juggle." We saw Tasso perform at the age of 79. He's still juggling and tossing teacups from foot to head (although no longer on a slack wire), but the reason he was our family's favorite act of the show was his comedy. We were created to work, to influence, to make a difference in the lives of those around us. Keep at this as long as you have strength.

#7: Keep ARC in mind

Achieve: What are the two or three things you are committed to achieving before you step away? These should be your areas of focus and help to prioritize your efforts as the clock ticks down.

Release: What are the things you wanted to achieve, dreamed of achieving, believed you needed to achieve that you now recognize will not happen (at least not under your leadership)? Release those things so that you can focus on what you need to achieve.

Clear: Spend your political capital clearing the decks for your successor. What are the challenges, structural reorganizations, personnel decisions, and unpopular changes you can make to clear the way for your successor, to improve his chances of success?

#8: Life is rarely like Ohio State vs. Purdue (Oct 20, 2012)

My son and I attended the Ohio State vs. Purdue football game on Saturday, Oct 20, 2012. Ohio State was ranked #7 in the nation and was 7-0 coming into the game. Purdue was unranked and was 3-3. In its previous two games, the Boilermakers had given up 82 points while scoring only 27. Yet it took a last-second touchdown and two-point conversion for Ohio State's backup quarterback, Kenny Guiton, to force overtime. It was a thrilling end to a terrible game for us Buckeyes.

Few people get the opportunity to experience a terrible life that turns around and ends well at the very last moment. Unfortunately, it is not that unusual for people to take a great life and to cap it off with a legacy-destroying last act. Make sure you end well. The key to this is recognizing that we are each bit players who have our opportunity to impact those around us for some combination of good and ill. Transition well. End well.

Questions to consider:

1. What transition is on your horizon? How are you preparing for it today? Which of the eight principles should be a focus for you at this time?

2. As you consider your next transition, what have you learned from past experience to help make it a positive one?

3. What opportunities might you have today to help others transition well?

Conclusion

Are You a Leader?

I hope you've found your "one thing" that made this book worth reading (see "Authors, Audience, and Purpose" for a reminder of that goal). I began this book by saying, "This book is intended for you who are pursuing the calling of leadership and challenges you to become the leader you'd love to follow." I also noted that as you read the chapters and answered the questions, that process might confirm that you are a leader and could help you identify areas for growth. At the same time, you may now realize you are not a leader, perhaps a follower with influence, and that you need to identify those leaders you'd love to follow. "Find your calling, be it leader or follower, and pursue it." Are you clearer about your calling? Are you a leader? Are you committed to pursuing the work of leaders: Crafting vision, building alignment, and driving execution?

What's next? Perhaps you should reread the book with someone else, holding each other accountable to answer the questions honestly and with a commitment to professional and personal growth. Perhaps you should give the book as a gift to a young leader who needs encouragement along the journey, or as a gift to a more senior leader who is considering the next chapter and whether success has been achieved or is still achievable. I'd love to have you buy our next book in the Become Collection: *Become the Manager You Wish You Had.*

A special note from Stephen: I'd love to hear from you! Send a note, write a review, give me a call at Julian Consulting. If I can help or encourage you, I'd be honored to see if there is a fit between the coaching and consulting I provide and the needs that you have. If you are looking for a speaker for your next retreat, annual conference, or other event, look no further. My website is www.julianconsulting.org and my e-mail address is stephen@julianconsulting.org. Reach out today to see how I can be of service to you and those you lead.

My dad has a small plaque hanging in his bathroom where he sees it each day as he prepares to reenter the world. It reads: "Lord, help me to finish well." So many leaders fail that final test. Let's commit to one another that we will be among those who finish well! Until we cross paths again, may you be blessed as you are a blessing to others!

91176153R00117

Made in the USA
San Bernardino, CA
23 October 2018